ANSELM

THE CROSSROAD SPIRITUAL LEGACY SERIES

ANSELM

The Joy of Faith

William H. Shannon

A Crossroad Book
The Crossroad Publishing Company
New York

Grateful acknowledgment is made to the following for permission to reprint previously published material:

The Life of Anselm, Archbishop of Canterbury, by Eadmer, edited with introductory notes and translation by R. W. Southern, 1972, Oxford Medieval Series, reprinted with permission of Oxford University Press, Oxford, England.
St. Anselm and His Biographer, by Richard W. Southern, 1963, reprinted with permission of Cambridge University Press, North American Branch, New York.
St. Anselm: A Portrait in a Landscape, by Richard W. Southern, 1990, reprinted with permission of Cambridge University Press, North American Branch, New York.
The Letters of Saint Anselm of Canterbury, 3 vols., translated and annotated by Walter Fröhlich, Kalamazoo, Mich., Cistercian Publications. Used with permission.
"The Coming" from the *Poems of R. S. Thomas.* Reprinted by permission of the University of Arkansas Press. Copyright 1985 by R. S. Thomas.

The Crossroad Publishing Company
370 Lexington Avenue, New York, NY 10017

Printed in the United States of America

Library of Congress Cataloging-in-Publication Data

Shannon, William Henry, 1917-
    Anselm : the joy of faith / William H. Shannon.
      p.   cm. – (The Crossroad spiritual legacy series)
    Includes bibliographical references.
    ISBN 0-8245-2513-2 (pbk.)
    1. Anselm, Saint, Archbishop of Canterbury, 1033-1109.
    2. Spirituality – History of doctrines – Middle Ages, 600-1500.
    I. Title II. Series.
BX4700.A58S57 1999
282'.092 – dc21
[B]   98-35090

1 2 3 4 5 6 7 8 9 10   04 03 02 01 00 99

To
Marie, Barbara, Frank, Sue
and All the Staropoli Family

Contents

Introduction

Anselm, both as a thinker and as a personality, is one of the rare significant figures who belong to all time, one to whom philosophers and historians and innumerable readers will turn for enlightenment and counsel....   — DAVID KNOWLES

It all began in Canterbury in 1983. I was visiting Canon A. M. Allchin, who was at the time canon residentiary at the cathedral. Walking about the town one day, I came upon a place of irresistible attraction: a bookstore. I went in. I bought one book. Its title was *Anselm and His Biographer,* and its author was R. W. Southern. I am not sure why I bought it, except perhaps that I was in Anselm's territory. He had been archbishop here. But that had been 890 years ago. I didn't even understand the title of the book, as at the time I had no idea what biographer of Anselm Southern was writing about. Nor did I know that Sir Richard W. Southern was and is the most distinguished of Anselmian scholars. What I did know at the time was that I had to buy that book. As I walked out of the bookstore, book in hand, I thought to myself: "Someday this book will be important to me."

Two years later, in 1985, I was invited to give the Otto Shults Distinguished Scholar Lectures at St. Bernard's Institute. The day chosen for the lectures was April 21. The feast of St. Anselm! Immediately I thought of that book which had been gathering dust on my shelves for the past two years. Of course! I could lecture on Anselm! But it was not to be! I was told: "No, people want you to speak on Thomas Merton." Reluctantly I put *Anselm and His Biographer* back on the shelf. It remained there till the spring of 1997, when I signed a contract with Crossroad Publishing Company to write a book on Anselm for their Spiritual Legacy series. My intuition at Canterbury — that someday

Southern's book would be important to me — had at long last been confirmed.

What drew me to want to write a book about Anselm? Probably there are a number of reasons. Most important would be the fact that he was a holy man. His whole life was a search for God: a God whom he had already found in a faith that was as unshakable as that of Moses at the burning bush. Yet like Moses he dared to approach the burning bush, and in words set afire there, he put into words his experience of God.

That experience came early to him. In a touching story of his childhood which he told to Eadmer, his biographer (the biographer I didn't know about when I purchased *Anselm and His Biographer* in Canterbury), Anselm speaks of his "meeting with God" on the top of a mountain. Aosta, the place where he was born, was a small Italian town nestled at the foot of a range of the Alps known as Jupiter. The mountains were so high that the young Anselm concluded that God's court must be at the top of them. One night in a dream he climbed the mountain and sure enough came to the court of God. As he climbed the slopes he saw reapers carelessly gathering the corn. He resolved to report their negligence to God. Arriving at God's court, he found God alone with his steward. He sat down at God's feet and the steward brought dazzlingly bright white bread (not the coarse black bread of the country folk) for the boy to eat. The next morning he confidently told his parents that he had seen God.

This childhood dream — one that any child in similar circumstances could have experienced — is a kind of parable of his life: the simplicity and directness of his passionate search for God, his fastidious horror of sin, but — most important of all — the confidence and clarity of his faith.

More than anything else, I think, what attracted me to write about Anselm was precisely that unbounded confidence he had in the faith he professed. It was a faith that in his adult life he would submit to rational examination. But he would do it with relish and joy and complete serenity. He had no anxieties that the whole system might fall apart if reason looked too closely at what faith believed. Faith was a gift from God; so was reason. How could they possible be in conflict, if faith was correctly understood and reason properly applied?

An age like ours, dominated as it is by science and technology, needs a good dose of confident and serene faith: not
only in God, but also in people, in the fundamental goodness
of life. We need a faith that tells us that each of us matters,
that we are important, that life is not just a jumble of unrelated
and meaningless events. Life holds together a context of related events that are going somewhere and have some kind of
ultimate meaning.

A Christmas editorial by Joan Beck expresses well the con-
temporary need for faith. She writes:

> To believe is scary, to accept a need to open our eyes to
> new possibilities, to become better than we are, to care for
> others more than we do, to acknowledge a power higher
> than ourselves and a will beyond our own.
>
> But not to believe is scarier, to listen to those who insist
> we are only a biological accident on a minor planet in a
> cold and pitiless universe and that good or evil, loving and
> loved, we will spend eternity as forgotten dust.[1]

Recently I saw the movie *Contact,* starring Jodi Foster as an
ardent young scientist who will accept nothing on faith. She demands hard data. Everything must be verified by facts. Since
her childhood, she had an intense interest in discovering some
data that might establish the existence of intelligent life else-
where in the universe. Might this perhaps be, one wonders, an
unconscious yearning on her part for a glimpse of the transcendent? At any rate, she has the opportunity of being involved in
a possible mission to the distant celestial body, Vega. The mission fails, but in its very failure she has an experience that she
cannot explain. She has made "contact." To a board of question-
ers she admits that she has no hard data for what happened. But
she has learned that life is precious, and that something greater
than hard data does indeed exist. Does this experience blossom
into faith? It's not clear if the movie meant to say that it did.
One thing is clear: she came to realize that the sharp contrast

---

1. Editorial page, *Rochester Democrat and Chronicle,* December 25, 1997.

she had been accustomed to make between scientific standards of evidence and religious faith had collapsed.

The movie, though hardly a great one, does make clear that today for many people faith is difficult to come by. One of the problems of our society is that we live in a culture that tends to make us one-dimensional people: content (or, worse still, condemned) to live on the surface of life with scarcely any sounding of life's depths. The violence in our cities, the exploitation of the Third World, the poverty that haunts our American land of plenty — these are so many signs of a one-dimensional society that has lost the ability to see and to care. So much media coverage — with its brief segments of factual information, but with scarcely any attempt to submit such information to the scrutiny of moral discourse in which values are seriously discussed — also signals a culture that is morally and spiritually bankrupt because it has become one-dimensional.

St. Anselm, with the serene confidence of his faith and his equally confident trust in human reason, is very much a two-dimensional person who can help us to see beyond the surface to the transcendent dimension in human life. With his guidance we may be able to glimpse Gerard Manley Hopkins's world "charged with the grandeur of God." We may discover with Elizabeth Barrett Browning that

> Earth's crammed with heaven,
> And every common bush afire with God
> And only they who see take off their shoes;
> The rest sit round it and pluck blackberries.

A society of blackberry pluckers needs to listen to the wisdom embodied in the writings of a man like Anselm. It is the intent of this book to open up that wisdom to people who may never have heard of Anselm, but who know all too well what it means to sit around and pluck blackberries.

❖

Whatever may be the reaction to this book, I am quite confident that it will not be: "What? Another book on Anselm?" Many of my friends, when they heard I had started work on a new book, asked me what the topic was. I told them I was writing about Anselm, a medieval saint who deserved to be better known. They were a bit skeptical, yet curious, wanting to know: who in the world is *he?* When I told them he was a saint who lived and wrote in the eleventh century, the reaction I got was: what possible significance could he have for us living in the last years of the twentieth century? These are the two questions I hope this book will answer. I want, first of all, to tell briefly his story, placing him in his historical setting and then, second, to discuss in a substantive way the lasting and sometimes brilliant contribution he has made to Christian thought. I hope to show the reader that he or she will be intellectually and spiritually enriched by contact with the writings of this impressive monk and archbishop of the eleventh century.

I should make clear to the reader that St. Anselm wrote in Latin, the common language of his time. This means that all of his writings will appear here in translation. The translations of the letters of Anselm, which you will find mostly in chapter 3, are taken from *The Letters of St. Anselm,* translated by Walter Fröhlich in three volumes and published by Cistercian Press. For Eadmer's *Vita Anselmi (The Life of Anselm)* I have used the translation made by R. W. Southern and for his *Recent Events in English History* that of Geoffrey Bosanquet. Otherwise the translations in this book are my own. After each of my own translations, I give the reference to the standard Latin text, which is that of F. S. Schmitt. The references will read as follows: S.=Schmitt's text; upper case Roman numerals will indicate the volume in Schmitt in which this text is located; the Arabic numeral will indicate the page in that volume. Thus S. I, 56 will mean: Schmitt, volume 1, page 56. The *Cur Deus Homo,* which is discussed in chapter 4, is divided into two books. This division I will indicate by lower case Roman numerals. Thus S. III, i, 19 means Schmitt, volume 3, part 1, page 19. Those who wish to check other translations will find them referred to in the Bibliography.

Part One

The Life
and Times of
St. Anselm

The Setting: The Eleventh Century

It is no exaggeration, I think, to say that Anselm was without doubt the most original thinker in an age when Christian thought was beginning to move in new and excitingly different directions. He was neither a follower of a system of thought nor a founder of one. He was his own person. And a charming person he was. His writings display the engaging personality that won the hearts of so many people in his own day and in later generations. Born in 1033, he died in 1109. Thus most of his life was lived in the eleventh century. It was, to say the least, an interesting century. It was a time when national boundaries were not yet clearly established. Someone Italian born could move easily in French society and just as easily in English. Christendom existed. Though it was not always "Christian," it served as a kind of religio-cultural backdrop against which a person could feel at home anywhere in Europe (unless he or she was Jewish or Muslim). It was this sense of being at home everywhere that encouraged people to move about a good deal more than might be expected in an age without planes, railroads, busses, automobiles: the comfortable ways of traveling that people today take for granted.

It was an exciting century too. It witnessed the proclamation of the "peace of God" (a wonderful ideal that never quite worked) and the victory of William the Conqueror in the battle of Hastings (an event that did work, making a lasting imprint on what British life and culture would be). Leif Ericson came to America (at least so it is thought). Macbeth murdered Duncan, king of Scotland (an event that Shakespeare would later immortalize in drama). The papacy was in deep trouble early in the century (the pawn of feuding Roman families), yet reached its zenith of power in 1073 when Hildebrand, Gregory VII, took possession of the papal throne and made it into an absolute monarchy, with supreme power, both spiritual and political. The saddest event of this century, I daresay, was the permanent split (1054) between Eastern and Western Christianity, with the subsequent loss to each of the enrichment that could come from the other. It was the age of the Holy Roman Empire aptly described by Edward Gibbon as neither holy, nor Roman, nor an empire. The century ended with the First Crusade taking possession of Jerusalem and setting up the Kingdom of Jerusalem, with Baldwin I as king. Another *fin-de-siècle* event — perhaps the more important in the long term — was the foundation at Citeaux of the reformed Benedictines known as the Cistercians. (The Cistercians remain a vital spiritual force in today's world. In March 1998 hundreds of Cistercians gathered at Citeaux to mark the nine hundredth anniversary of their foundation.)

It was an age in which monasteries played a crucial civilizing role in a culture that often was uncivilized. They were centers of prayer and guardians of culture. They were "publishers" of books at a time when books had to be patiently copied by hand. They offered "bed and breakfast" accommodations to travelers and scholars who moved about from place to place. They anticipated the great universities of the next century as places of education and learning.

Theology was on the brink of dramatic changes. New ways of talking about God and Christian faith were beginning to emerge. Christian writers heretofore had contented themselves with collecting texts from the Scriptures and the church fathers, reflecting on them and attempting to resolve what might appear to be conflicting or contradictory statements. Scriptures and authority were the final arbiters of Christian faith. The eleventh century began looking to other ways of reflecting on the things of God. Reason and the dialectical tools of grammar and logic came increasingly into use for understanding the truths of faith. It was, as Gordon Leff put it, "the first age of reason's new-found voice."[1] And in this new enterprise Anselm was unquestionably the leader.

It was an approach that promised new riches, yet it posed questions never faced before. Is fallible human reason qualified to deal with matters revealed by God? Or, to ask the more ominous question, can the truths of faith stand up to the critique of reason? Those who saw the dangers of this new direction could point to Berengar (1000–1088). He wrote about the Eucharist. Though there is some obscurity about his teaching, he seems to have argued that, in the eucharistic celebration, reason sees bread and wine both before and after the words: "This is my Body. . . . This is my Blood." There cannot, therefore, be a physical change in the elements. The change that takes place is a spiritual one (perhaps a change in the attitude of the participants?). What he taught squared with neither Scripture nor authority. He was condemned by several synods. He recanted and died in communion with the church. There was no assurance, however, that others would be so docile.

But if the approach through reason could lead in wrong directions, it could also be a source of faith enrichment. I hope to show that Anselm's writings are proof of this. Anselm, as we shall see, knew well how to put reason at the service of faith. And he did it, as I have already suggested, with great confidence and with a sense of joy.

---

1. Leff, *Medieval Thought from St. Augustine to Ockham*, 98. Full publication data for references is provided in the bibliography beginning on p. 187.

The Persons

ANSELM (1033–1109): more about his story later.

ERMENBERGA: his mother, a native of Aosta, an ancient Roman town on the southern boundary of the kingdom of Burgundy.

GUNDULF: his father, from Lombardy.

RICHEZA: his sister, whom Anselm provided for after her husband failed to return from the crusade. Her son, named for his uncle, but with none of his uncle's brilliance of mind, became, through Anselm's influence, abbot of Bury St. Edmund's. He made a name for himself as one of the earliest defenders of the Immaculate Conception of the Blessed Virgin Mary.

LANFRANC (ca. 1010–89): a brilliant scholar and teacher, prior of the monastery of Bec in Normandy (when Anselm first met him), appointed in 1070 as archbishop of Canterbury. His renown attracted Anselm to enter the monastery of Notre Dame of Bec.

WILLIAM (ca. 1027–87): duke of Normandy. Defeated the Anglo-Saxons at the battle of Hastings (1066) and became William I, king of England.

WILLIAM II (d. 1100): son and, in 1087, successor of William I as king of England. He is often referred to as William Rufus, because of his ruddy complexion. Southern describes him as "that ogre among medieval kings."[2]

HENRY I (ca. 1068–1135): youngest son of William I, succeeded his brother. He is also called Henry Beauclerc, because he could write.

ROBERT OF MEULAN (ca. 1046–1118): advisor to William II and Henry I, a man of astute political skill and power. He and Anselm were often at odds with one another on matters of church and state.

EADMER (ca. 1060–ca. 1130): biographer of Anselm. From his infancy a monk of the monastery of Christ's Church, Canterbury. He first met Anselm in 1079 when, as the recently appointed abbot of Bec, Anselm came to Canterbury to check on the lands owned by the monastery. When in 1093 Anselm became the archbishop of Canterbury, Eadmer became his sec-

---

2. Luscombe and Evans. *Anselm: Aosta, Bec, and Canterbury*, 29.

retary and ardent admirer. For the next sixteen years they were constantly together. Eadmer began writing down what he saw and heard of the archbishop, as well as the reminiscences of his past that Anselm often shared. For a time Anselm even read the text and offered corrections. Then one day, deciding that he was too unworthy to have his life story written, he ordered Eadmer to destroy it. Obedient to the letter, but hardly to the spirit of his archbishop's command, Eadmer destroyed the manuscript, but only after he had made a copy. As every writer knows, it's not easy for an author to destroy his own manuscript, and we can be grateful that as a result of Eadmer's gentle dissembling, the *Vita Anselmi* survived. For some twenty years Eadmer kept his disobedience secret; finally he unburdened his deep sense of guilt to Archbishop Ralph, Anselm's successor as archbishop of Canterbury. Ralph ordered him to record in the *Vita Anselmi* what he had done. Eadmer did so. After telling of his disobedience, he begs his readers that, if his work proves pleasing to them, they "deign to intercede for this and for my other sins, lest the weight of them so hold me down that I am unable to come to him whose life and deeds I have however crudely described" (*Vita Anselmi*, 151).

POPE GREGORY VII (1020–85; pope: 1073–85): originally Hildebrand, born of humble parentage in Tuscany, served the reform popes Nicholas II and Alexander II and accentuated the reforms after his own election by popular acclaim in 1073. He prohibited clerical marriages and lay investiture. His exalted mystique of the papacy is set forth in his *Dictatus papae* (1075), which proclaimed the supreme power of the pope: his right to depose all princes, temporal and spiritual, his sole right to be called universal pastor. The pope can judge all, but he can be judged by no one.

POPE URBAN II (ca. 1035–99; pope: 1088–99): became pope at a time when the antipope Clement III claimed the papal throne. He had difficulties with William II of England, who did not recognize him as legitimate pope until 1095. In 1098 Pope Urban welcomed Anselm to Rome and housed him in the Lateran palace.

POPE PASCHAL II (pope: 1099–1118): in conflict with Henry I over the question of lay investiture. A weak, vacillating pope under whom the power of the papacy was diminished.

MATILDA, countess of Tuscany (1046–1115): supporter of Pope Gregory VII in his conflict with the Holy Roman emperors. Anselm sent her a copy of his *Prayers and Meditations.*

GAUNILO: a monk of Marmoutier near Tours, he challenged Anselm's *Proslogion,* specifically his argument for the existence of God. Anselm replied to him and had Gaunilo's comment and his rejoinder copied with the text of the *Proslogion.*

BOSO: a young monk who came to Bec during Anselm's last years as abbot. He acted as partner in dialogue with, and sometimes as critic of, Anselm's teachings about redemption in the *Cur Deus Homo.*

ROSCELIN: an itinerant teacher in the rapidly growing expression of intellectual life coming into existence in the secular (as distinguished from the monastic) schools. He mistakenly claimed that his teaching on the Trinity (which was clearly heretical) was supported by Anselm.

The Life

Aosta, the place of Anselm's birth (1033) was an ancient Roman city in Burgundy on the border of Lombardy. Founded by the Emperor Augustus and bearing his name, it nestles at the foot of the lofty Alps near the St. Bernard Pass.

His mother, Ermenberga, a native Burgundian, was a pious woman whose life and teaching sowed in him the seeds of that passion for God that, after a misspent youth, more and more defined his life. When he was about fifteen, Anselm wanted to enter a monastery, but his father would not allow him to do so. After his mother's death, his desire for the religious life cooled little by little. As Eadmer describes it: "He began to desire to go the way of the world rather than to leave the world for a monastic life" (*Vita Anselmi,* 4). Eadmer is not very clear on what it meant to "go the way of the world." He speaks of his giving himself up to "worldly amusements." "The ship of his heart had as it were lost its anchor and drifted almost entirely among the waves of the world" (ibid.). A tantalizing metaphor, to be sure, but we are left to imagine what precisely it meant. At any rate, in about 1056, after a quarrel with his father, with whom he seemed never to have been on good terms, he left Aosta never to return.

Crossing the mountains, accompanied by a servant, he suddenly grew weak and faint. He tried to revive himself by eating snow, as there was nothing to eat. So they thought at least, till the servant opened the bag they were carrying and found in it some bread "of exceptional whiteness" (to use Eadmer's words, obviously recalling Anselm's childhood dream). After three years in Burgundy and France, Anselm made his way to Normandy and the monastery at Bec. A Benedictine monastery founded by Hirluin in 1034 (the year after Anselm's birth), Bec prospered under the patronage of the dukes of Normandy. It was Lanfranc who brought that patronage when, as prior of Bec, he became chief counselor in religious matters to William, Duke of Normandy. Already famous as a teacher of the liberal arts, he made Bec a center of learning unrivaled in Europe. He taught not only the young monks, but also sons of the nobility who sought a good education for their children.

Lanfranc had come to Bec about 1042. Anselm arrived to study with him in 1060, when Bec's prior was at the height of his considerable ability and influence. As a Benedictine novice, Anselm would have received Lanfranc's instructions about the Rule of St. Benedict and the spirituality which that Rule embodies. Anselm was always grateful to his teacher, whose reputation had brought him to Bec in the first place. They were together at Bec scarcely three years. Lanfranc became abbot of the monastery of Caen in 1063 and seven years later archbishop of Canterbury. Anselm succeeded him as prior and in 1078 was elected as the second abbot of Bec.

By 1078 Anselm had written some of his most important writings: some letters, the early prayers and meditations, as well as the *Monologion* and the *Proslogion*. It was the latter two that made quite clear his departure in theological methodology from his famous teacher. Lanfranc belonged to the patristic tradition for which theology, as I pointed out earlier, amounted to analyzing texts from Scripture and the fathers. Anselm was moving in a new direction, turning confidently to human reason to help him understand what he believed in faith.

The sixteen years he spent as abbot of Bec were probably

the happiest years of his life. He experienced great joy in the tranquillity of the cloister. Some of his most influential writings come from this period and were written at the request of his monks. Deeply committed to the monastic routine, he loved talking to the monks of Bec. It is also clear that they enjoyed listening to him. He did his best to draw them into dialogue. In fact to help them to do this well, he wrote his first book, the *De Grammatico*. As the title suggests, it was a book on grammar concerned with words and sentences, definitions and analyses: necessary, though hardly exciting, topics to write about. Its aim was to teach his pupils to read, to write — but, more than that, to think, speak, and write clearly and logically. It was important that his students, if they were to enter meaningfully into dialogue, be able to distinguish the true from the false, the illusory from the real. They had to learn how important it was to pierce through words and to go beyond the appearances of things in order to get at the reality which they partly reveal and partly conceal. For Anselm the *De Grammatico* was the beginning of a journey that would lead to the argument of the *Proslogion*. There he will reach beyond words, beyond appearances, even beyond created reality to the ultimate reality of God.

In 1092 he was forced to deal with a potentially damaging criticism. Roscelin, an itinerant scholar who apparently caused dissension wherever he went, presented an understanding of the Trinity that was obviously heterodox. This need not have involved Anselm except that Roscelin had cited Anselm and Lanfranc as supporters of his view. Roscelin claimed that if the three persons of the Trinity are one thing and not three things, then both the Father and the Holy Spirit must have become incarnate along with the Son. Anselm rejected Roscelin's position and expressed his adherence to the Christian creeds. While still abbot of Bec, Anselm began a reply, which he did not complete till the year following his consecration as archbishop. The reply was actually in the form of a letter sent to Pope Urban II, hence its title *Epistola de Incarnatione Verbi* (*Epistle on the Incarnation of the Word*) in which he defends the belief of the church, expressed in the early councils, that it was the Word, and only the Word, that became incarnate.

As abbot of Bec he made several trips to England to see after the lands and properties there that belonged to the abbey. In 1092 he wrote to the monastery at Bec, telling Baldric, the prior, and the community that he would be delayed in returning from his third trip of inspection, because King William II refused to allow him to leave. Instead Anselm was forcibly invested with the archbishopric of Canterbury on March 6, 1093. (The see had been vacant for four years after the death of Lanfranc, and William had been receiving the revenues that belonged to the church.) Now on his deathbed, in fear of imminent death, William chose Anselm to be archbishop. Anselm would have nothing of it. But bishops and nobles, present in the sick room, pressed the episcopal crozier into his clenched fist and brought him to the nearby chapel where they joyfully began chanting the *Te Deum.* Anselm reproached them: "Do you realize what it is you are trying so hard to do? You are trying to harness together under one yoke an untamed bull and an old and feeble sheep." (Anselm was sixty years old at the time.) Despite the irregularities of his investiture and his profuse protestations of his unworthiness, Anselm would eventually accept the office of archbishop of Canterbury.

A letter sent to him by Osbern, a monk of Christchurch, Canterbury, who had spent some time with Anselm at Bec, strongly urged him to accept the office of archbishop. Osbern warns him not to tempt God. For God, he says, has given him the greatest possible signs of the divine will calling him to acceptance. He describes these signs in graphic detail.

> How could God more clearly show to you who were to be elected that you were indeed to be promoted than by causing the king, noble because of his victories, formidable by his severity to all, to have taken to his bed, sick even unto death; and having promoted you, he immediately revived, regained his strength, and from being cruel and inhuman, became the mildest and most gentle of men? What, I ask you, could be more congenial to the result or more favorable to your integrity than the sight of you being dragged violently before the bed of the sick man, your right hand shamelessly pulled out of your bosom by the right hands of others, your left hand forcefully held

back lest it help its sister, the staff cruelly thrust between
thumb and index finger since the rest of your fingers were
stubbornly held closed, and, after that, being lifted bodily
from the ground and carried to the church on the arms of
the bishops, where you continued to cry out and to resist
strongly those forcing you, until the *Te Deum* was sung?

(Letter 149, *Letters*, 2:12–13)

What Osbern saw as the disposition of divine providence,
some of the monks of Bec viewed as a betrayal on Anselm's
part of his stability at Bec. Reluctantly they gave their assent.
Anselm writes to them in the late summer of 1093.

Although divine providence does not separate me from your
bodily presence without great spiritual pain to my heart, yet I
pray to the Lord that the love he has given, by which my soul
embraces you in its depths, may remain imperishable.

(Letter 156, *Letters*, 2:28–36)

He understands the sadness they might experience about his
departure. He makes clear to them that their unhappiness about
his leaving weighs him down more heavily than any earthly
riches or ecclesiastical distinctions might console him. He is
deeply wounded that some of the monks believe that it was
greed rather than religious necessity that motivated him in
accepting the archbishopric. He writes:

If my life and conduct do not satisfy these people, I do not
know how else I can persuade them what is in my conscience in this matter. I have already lived for thirty-three
years in the habit of a monk, three years without office, fifteen years as prior, and the same number as abbot, in such a
way that all good people who know me love me, not through
my own efforts but through the workings of God's grace, and
this is especially true of those who know me closely and
personally.

He makes clear to them that, were he free to do so, he would
prefer to "serve and obey as a monk under a superior." Yet he

does not see how he could without sin refuse the responsibility that has been thrust upon him. He speaks of his monastic profession. "When I professed myself a monk, I denied myself to myself, so that from then on I would not belong to myself." He begs them not to love him less because he is following what he sees as God's will for him. "I do not see," he tells them, "how I can take myself away from the church of the English without resisting God." He commends them to the Lord Jesus Christ, to St. Mary, St. Peter, and St. Benedict. "By the merits and intercessions of the saints, may he who redeemed you with his blood be your abbot and your guardian and grant you to live happily in his kingdom after this life" (Letter 156, 2:28–35).

Thus it was that with a heavy heart he finally acquiesced and was consecrated archbishop and primate of all Britain on December 4, 1093. He would continue in office until his death on April 21, 1109. By inclination and talent Anselm was a better monk and writer than administrator. Moreover his unpromising beginning as archbishop heralded what was to be a stormy career which would see him twice in exile.

Anselm's understanding of his tasks as archbishop was quite different from the way most other bishops and archbishops of his time looked upon their office. Increasingly they came to see themselves as administrators. For Anselm his first responsibility was to the monastic community at Canterbury. That community was his charge and his joy. He also felt it his duty to defend the rights and privileges that belonged to the church of Canterbury. These he saw as rights and privileges that ultimately belonged to the heavenly kingdom. A further responsibility was to define and expound the doctrinal and moral teachings of the church. But the duties, which were external to his monastic community, were never allowed to replace his continuing search for a deeper understanding of faith or his constant prayer, alone with God or in union with the monks of Christchurch, Canterbury.

Scarcely had he taken office as archbishop than he was in trouble with King William II. William insisted on giving him the pallium (the cape of lamb's wool given by the pope to archbishops as the symbol of their office). Anselm refused, insisting that he go to Rome to receive it from Pope Urban II. William

Rufus would have nothing of it and had the pallium sent from Rome. Anselm finally compromised by taking the pallium from the altar at Canterbury Cathedral. This disagreement was only a beginning: further conflict arose almost immediately over Anselm's demands for reform of the English church in accordance with the reforms instituted in the church by Pope Gregory VII. William, who had recovered from his sickness (as Anselm had predicted he would), refused the archbishop's demands and, supported by his adviser Robert Count of Meulan, would not allow Anselm to go to Rome to discuss the matter with the pope. Anselm, determined to defend the rights of the church, set off for the continent, threatening to walk to Rome naked and barefoot if need be. He was not allowed to return to England while William lived. His exile lasted from November 1097 to September 1100.

After leaving England, he traveled through Burgundy and on December 23 arrived at the abbey of Cluny, where he was received with joy and reverence. From Cluny he went to Lyons, where his friend Hugh was archbishop. Worn out by the strain of continuous conflict and exhausted from his journeying, he was grateful for Hugh's insistence that he stay and rest awhile. He remained there for some weeks.

During Passion week, traveling incognito with two other monks, he at last arrived in Rome. Pope Urban II received him with joy and ordered that he be lodged in the Lateran palace. Eventually leaving Rome, he stayed in several monasteries in Italy, during which time he completed the *Cur Deus Homo* (*Why God Became Human*), which he had begun in England. His partner in the dialogue of this work was Boso, a young monk whom Anselm had taught at Bec and in whom he recognized a special aptitude for philosophy. When he began this book on God's redemptive action, he earnestly requested the abbot of Bec to release Boso, as he felt the need of this young monk to help him with his writing. Boso is given a special role in the dialogue of teacher and disciple that makes up the *Cur Deus Homo*.

More than once Anselm asked Pope Urban to relieve him of his pastoral responsibilities as archbishop of Canterbury. According to Eadmer's account, the pope listened to his request and then exclaimed in astonishment: "Bishop! Shepherd! You have not yet suffered bloodshed, nor wounds! Are you already seeking to steal away from the care of the Lord's sheepfold?"[3] The pope refused his request, but promised to write to King William. Meantime he invited Anselm to speak at the Council of Bari (October 1098) on the teaching of the Western church that the Holy Spirit proceeded from the Father and the Son and not just from the Father, as the Eastern church taught (and still does). The council fathers, hearing of King William's unjust treatment of the archbishop of Canterbury, was prepared to excommunicate him. Anselm implored that they not do so. His counsel prevailed and, as Eadmer put it, all were in admiration of this good bishop who was so ready to return good for evil.

In the third year of his exile, word came to him at Lyons that King William had died. Soon after, the new king, Henry I, wrote to him entreating him to return, promising him that he and the whole kingdom would submit to his advice and direction. Anselm came back to Canterbury. Almost immediately, despite the king's promise, problems arose over the investiture of bishops by the king. Henry wanted Anselm to receive the archbishopric from him. In addition, the king insisted on retaining the power of investing other bishops with the symbols of their office. Fresh from the Council of Bari, which had affirmed the church's strong position against lay investiture, Anselm refused. If the king insisted, the archbishop would have no choice but to excommunicate the king and any bishops who received investiture from the royal hands. The king's unwillingness to give up what he considered ancestral rights forced Anselm into a second exile that lasted from December 1103 to September 1106.

In 1103 William of Warelwast was sent by Henry to Rome to seek from Pope Paschal either cancellation or mitigation of the decrees against lay investiture. He failed to achieve either. William did, however, visit Anselm in Lyons, where once again the archbishop of Canterbury was staying with his friend, Archbishop Hugh. The king's messenger advised Anselm that the king would welcome him back to England, if "you return to him

---

3. Eadmer, *History of Recent Events in England,* 107.

on the understanding that you will treat him in all respects as your predecessors are known to have treated his predecessors." Anselm's response was simple and firm: "I reply that neither at my baptism nor at any of my ordinations did I promise to observe the law or the custom of your father or of Archbishop Lanfranc, but rather the law of God and of all the orders I have received" (Letter 319, *Letters*, 3:26).

In the spring of 1105 Pope Pascal wrote to Anselm informing him that at the Lenten synod of 1105 held in Rome, sentence of excommunication was promulgated against Count Robert of Meulan and likewise the bishops who had submitted to royal investiture. Sentence against King Henry, he said, had been deferred awaiting the arrival of messengers from him who were expected at Easter. Earlier the pope had written to the count of Meulan saying that he had come to understand that it was Robert who almost alone had been advising the king to resist the Roman decrees in the matter of investitures. Pope Paschal offered to remit his sins if he turned away from his evil ways. Robert's very age, the pope admonished him, should suggest a turning to God. (Robert had been with William the Conqueror in the battle of Hastings, so he was probably at this time in his sixties.)

Sobered by the news of what was about to happen and not overlooking the sad fate of sovereigns who had persisted in defying the church, Henry was ready to make concessions to the pope and the archbishop. A reconciliation of king and archbishop was achieved at l'Aigle in Normandy. Anselm lifted the excommunication of the count of Meulan, since he had promised to obey the Roman decrees.

By 1106 Anselm's health was strong enough that he was able to return to England. A royal welcome awaited him at Dover. Men and women of every rank crowded the beach at his arrival. There was special rejoicing at Christchurch, Canterbury, that their beloved shepherd had returned to his flock. In the short time of life that yet remained for him, Anselm and the king worked together, though not always in complete harmony, for the reform of the ecclesiastical scene in England. The restoration of ecclesiastical discipline was Anselm's last gift to the Church of England that had been entrusted to his care.

The Philosopher and Monk

Second only to Anselm's ardor for God was his enthusiasm for writing and for dealing with abstruse philosophical and theological issues. Subsequent ages have seen him as a philosopher. It is an appropriate description if one intends "philosophy" in a monastic sense. According to Jean Leclercq, the Greek fathers described the monastic life as "philosophy according to Christ" and "the only true philosophy."

> In the monastic middle ages, as well as in antiquity, *philosophia* designates, not a theory or way of knowing, but a lived wisdom, a way of living according to reason. There are, in effect, two ways of living according to reason. Either one lives according to worldly wisdom, as taught by pagan philosophers, and that is *philosophia saecularis* or *mundialis,* or one lives according to Christian wisdom which is not of this world but already of the world to come, and this is the *philosophia caelestis* or *spiritualis* or *divina.*[4]

However much he was philosopher and theologian, however much he is remembered by subsequent history for the famous "ontological argument for the existence of God," Anselm was first and foremost a monk. For most of his adult life his spirituality was nourished by the Rule of St. Benedict, whose only logic was the logic of daily life lived simply, in community, in obedience to the Gospel and in imitation of Christ. At Bec and at Canterbury he was happiest when he could be with his monks. "Just as an owl when she is in her hole with her chicks," he said to the monks of Christchurch, Canterbury, on one occasion, "so it is with me. For when I am with you, all is well with me, and this is the joy and consolation of my life." The monks of Bec and those of Canterbury held him in deep affection.

He was an exceedingly kind and compassionate father. The brutality that all too often marked monastic life, especially in the treatment of children, saw no place in the monasteries

---

4. Leclercq, *The Love of Learning and the Desire for God,* 128.

under his leadership. According to Eadmer, Anselm wrote to a certain abbot strongly opposing threats and blows as punitive measures for disciplining children. "Are they not human?" he asks. "Are they not flesh and blood like you? Would you like to have been treated as you treated them?" Southern has pointed out: "On no issue is he more remote from his age than in his opposition to the insensate brutality with which the monastic authorities — no doubt their imitation of the rest of the world in this — treated the children under their care."[5] His sensitivity even extended to animals. Eadmer remembered how on one occasion he had reined in his horse when a hare chased by dogs ran under it for protection and how he had spoken sharply to those who were laughing at the animal's plight. "You laugh, do you? There is no laughter for this poor unhappy beast." A caring, compassionate, thoughtful man, Anselm exemplified the picture of the abbot described in Rule 64 of the Rule of St. Benedict: "Let him strive to be loved rather than feared." In his book *The Evolution of Medieval Thought* Dom David Knowles has said that Anselm was "perhaps the nearest approach to the ideal abbot that the Benedictines ever saw" (99). A grand compliment indeed and one that would surely have pleased Anselm. What made the archbishopric difficult for him was the way the responsibilities of his office continually prevented him from living the simplicity of the monastic life in the company of the monks he loved. But he always felt sure of their love. He was able to write to the monks at Bec with a confidence born of experience, not of pride: "All good people who know me love me." Though it can be questioned whether or not he was a mystic, as Evelyn Underhill claimed him to be, "there can be no doubt that Anselm is first and foremost successor to the legacy of monasticism as well as to a certain mysticism that is characteristic of medieval thought. Put simply we could say that the difference between the later schoolmen and Anselm is precisely the difference between the university and the monastery."[6]

---

5. *St. Anselm and His Biographer*, 347–48.
6. Gregory Schufreider, *Confessions of a Rational Mystic*, 1.

Evelyn Underhill did indeed understand Anselm to be a mystic.[7] It would seem that Eadmer may well have agreed with her. Especially noteworthy is his description of Anselm standing at prayer enveloped by a ball of fire.

> One night when [Riculfus, the sacristan] was walking through the cloister waiting for the moment when he would waken the brethren for vigils, he happened to pass the door of the chapter house. He looked in and saw Anselm standing in prayer in the midst of a great ball of blazing fire. He was amazed and could not tell what this vision might portend, for he thought that Anselm would have been asleep at that hour rather than occupied in prayer. So he went quickly up to the dormitory and walked to Anselm's bed; but he found no trace of him there. Then he returned and found him in the chapter house, but without the ball of fire which had been there before he left.
>
> (*Vita Anselmi*, 25–26)

On his deathbed, when one might well expect him to be concerned about his relationship with God (since he so often called himself a wretched sinner), he was thinking, instead, of a book he had yet to write. When the brothers told him on Palm Sunday of 1109 that he was surely going to be at the Lord's court in heaven for Easter, he said he was ready to go if that was God's will. "However," he said, "if God would prefer me to remain among you, at least until I can settle a question about the origin of the soul, which I have been turning over in my mind, I will welcome this with gratitude" (*Vita Anselmi*, 142). Without guile but with great confidence in the abilities God had given him, he adds that God might want him to stay a bit longer, as he was not sure that after he was gone anyone else would be able to solve this problem. He went to his death with pen

---

7. In *Mystics of the Church* (Cambridge: James Clarke, 1975; first pub. 1925) Evelyn Underhill writes: "The fortunate survival of the Meditations of St. Anselm reveals the deep reservoirs of mystical devotion, the fervour, humility and love, which fed the active career of that great statesman and ecclesiastic" (74).

poised but the projected book unwritten. One wonders if anyone following him did actually deal with the question to his
satisfaction.[8]

On Tuesday of Holy Week, April 20, he was so weak that he
was unable to speak. Ralph, bishop of Rochester, asked him to
give his absolution and blessing to those who were present and
to the other people who lived under his authority, including the
king, the queen, and their children. He raised his hand in blessing. Early the next morning, as the monks were singing matins
in the cathedral, the book of the Gospels was brought to his
bedside. One of the monks read to him the passion narrative
that would be used in the Mass that day. When he came to the
words of Jesus: "You are they who have remained with me in
my temptations. And I appoint to you a kingdom, as my Father has appointed to me a kingdom, so that you may eat and
drink at my table in my kingdom," Anselm began to breathe
more slowly. The end had come. On April 21, 1109, as dawn
was breaking on the day before Holy Thursday, with his brother
monks gathered about him, in the sixteenth year of his tenure
as archbishop of Canterbury, in the seventy-sixth year of his life,
he passed "into the hands of his creator" (*Vita Anselmi*, 143).

---

8. Gilbert Crispin, who became abbot of Westminster, was one of Anselm's
most gifted disciples as well as a close friend. In his *De Anima* he attempted to
deal with Anselm's question (part of the question being: how can original sin
be transmitted from parent to child, if each soul is directly created by God?).
It seems that Crispin himself was not completely happy with his answer,
which makes one wonder if Anselm would have been satisfied with it (see
Southern, *St. Anselm: A Portrait in a Landscape*, 372, n.).

Part Two

The Spirituality of St. Anselm

Anselm appeared to his contemporaries to be preeminently a man of prayer, someone who walked with God and who could guide others in the same way. — BENEDICTA WARD

It is probably safe to say that today's readers who could claim some slight acquaintance with Anselm would identify him as the author of "the ontological argument" for the existence of God. This "argument," actually cast in the form of a prayer and appearing in his early work called the *Proslogion,* waited eight centuries before it acquired the descriptive adjective "ontological" (a gift from Immanuel Kant, who discussed the argument only to reject it). The fact that Kant was writing about it in the eighteenth century points to the astounding fact that a brief chapter in the *Proslogion,* not even a full page of text, had taken on a life of its own. Since Anselm's day, philosophers in almost every age have given thought to it: some accepting, others rejecting, but scarcely any age able completely to ignore it. In the twentieth century Karl Barth has strongly defended it. So has the "Ballad of St. Anselm," which I recently downloaded from the Internet! The "argument" continues to exercise its fascination with philosophers and theologians alike. And I dare to say that the reader will feel something of its spell when we discuss it later.

What I hope to do in what follows is to discuss some of the important writings of Anselm. It is not my intent to discuss these writings in detail. I have no thought of producing a scholarly work on Anselm because, first, I doubt I would be equal to the task, and, second, such scholarly works already exist. Those looking for this type of study would do better to turn to the writings of R. W. Southern, G. R. Evans, Benedicta Ward, Jasper Hopkins, M. J. Charlesworth, and Gregory Schufreider, to name but a few who represent the best in Anselmian scholarship.

My purpose is less ambitious, though perhaps in its own way more demanding. I want to present selections from Anselm's writings to today's readers, hoping to show that what he wrote nearly a thousand years ago can ring true in today's world. Though our economics, politics, industry, technology, and secular culture may seem to remove us far from the Europe of the eleventh century, still we find in him a humanity and a Christian faith that we share. The human questions about life and its meaning, joy and sorrow, God and faith, sin and freedom, Christ and redemption, human relationships and how to deal with them, violence and peace — these are questions that belong not to a particular age, but to a common humanity. Anselm dealt with these questions and it is helpful to us to hear what he said.

To express my purpose in another way: I want to distill from Anselm's writings the spirituality that I find there. The word "spirituality" calls for clarification. I have written several books belonging to this genre. They are books, such as *Silence on Fire*, which grew out of my reflection on the writings of Thomas Merton. I recall one day going into a local bookstore and, to my dismay, finding my books listed under the category of "Inspirational." That afternoon I called the manager of the store and pointed out to her that there was a growing interest in spirituality, that spirituality was a distinct genre of religious writing and did not at all fit into the category of "Inspirational." It ought to be properly named, I suggested, and have a place all of its own. The manager thanked me for my suggestion. But thus far nothing has changed. I am still in "Inspirational" — alien territory, alongside of self-help, pop psychology, "you-can-be-a-success-all-by-yourself" stories, and similar light-weight and sometimes lame-brain stuff. Oh, well, *c'est la vie!*

This experience suggests to me that, before I write about Anselm's spirituality, I would be well advised to clarify what the term means to me. When I speak about spirituality, I am not, in the first instance at least, talking about prayer or devotion or liturgy. I am talking about *life*. It is very wrong to think of our spirituality as a compartment of our lives to which we give attention on occasion. Spirituality is not something we "try to get in" in the midst of an otherwise hectic world. Spirituality has to do with our whole life — hectic and all — lived in its totality under the influence of God's Spirit. It is our whole life lived in the consciousness that we and our sisters and brothers and the whole world are sustained in existence from moment to moment by the loving goodness of God. Spirituality, in other words, is the realization that there is more to life than what you see. Topping the computer ad: "what you see is what you get," spirituality insists that you get more than you see. It is attuned to a world of reality below and above (indeed all around) our ordinary daily experience. It is this world that alone is truly real; yet those who are content to live simply on life's surface are completely oblivious of these wonders that exist within them and all around them. How mightily our lives are changed when we become aware of this other deeper dimension.

This dimension of interiority and inner depth is present in every one of us and can be reached (or, perhaps better, uncovered or recovered) by those who are willing to submit to the discipline which such a life demands. While this discipline may require a change in behavior (we have to deal with our sinfulness and our failures to live and do the truth), still its principal aim is to achieve a change in consciousness whereby we view reality differently. We discover God at the center of our very being and at the center of all reality. This discovery liberates us from selfishness, as we awake to the realization that apart from God we are nothing. We *are* only because we are in God. This is true of all of us and of all reality. All that is meets in God. Anselm prays this truth: "You are so great, Lord, that all things are filled with you and are in you" (S. I,

116). As sisters and brothers of the divine we see God in every human face.

It is the discovery of this dimension of human existence that makes life worth the living.

We live in an age of seekers: people who experience a sinking feeling that their lives are empty and aimless. Like Dante Alighieri, they find themselves "in a dark wood," where "the right way" seems to have been lost. The fare of "bread and circuses," which life on the surface of existence offers them, no longer satisfies. They search for meaning. They want to know if life leads anywhere. If it does, then where? If it doesn't, then not much matters.

Anselm writes with the confident conviction that life does have meaning. With the sure hand of a master teacher he disentangles life's confusions and leads us in the journey along the path of faith and reason. It is not always, he would readily admit, an easy journey to walk; but he is sure that it is the right one. He knows all too well the human weaknesses that hold us back on life's journey, the frailties that take us on fruitless detours, the meanness and violence that sometimes can blow up the road before us. In one of his prayers, he sums up in a single line the frustration that so often accompanies the search for God: "I was moving toward God and I got in my own way" (S. I, 99). Still the confident trust he has in God, who is his one great passion, never leaves him. The firm unhesitant faith that the grace of God can overcome all obstacles is an enduring reality in his life. He is sure of his footing. He is clear about the way to go. This will become evident, I believe, as we enter into the world of his writings.

Chapter 1

Learning to Pray
with St. Anselm

Anselm's first collection of Prayers has the interest which at-taches to the appearance of a new star in the heavens, and it exhibits all the qualities of forceful expression and a fresh view of the state of the human soul necessary for giving a new impetus to devotional literature. —R. W. SOUTHERN

Spirituality, as I have pointed out earlier, is by no means synonymous with prayer. For spirituality has to do with the total reality of our lives. Still I must hasten to make the fairly obvious point that prayer is an important element of that total reality and indeed needs to permeate it. For this reason I want to begin this study of Anselm's spirituality by talking about the meaning that prayer had for him.

Anselm wrote no systematic treatise on prayer. He did, however, write a book of prayers that was something of a sensation in his day (*The Prayers and Meditations*) and a book that is one long "theological" prayer (the mysterious and charming *Proslogion*). There is also the fact that Anselm was a monk, and one thing monks do is to pray. The prayers that Anselm wrote undoubtedly grew out of his own practice of *lectio divina,* or what we might call today prayerful "spiritual reading." Since he was a writer, it is not surprising that he would put some of his experience of prayer to manuscript.

Before discussing Anselm's understanding of prayer, I want to speak briefly about the place of reading and meditation (*lectio divina*) in the Rule of St. Benedict. The Rule, which Anselm would have studied as a novice and discoursed about with the monks of Bec when he became prior and later abbot, provided for periods of reading each day. It is helpful to understand what reading meant to St. Benedict in the fifth century and to Anselm some five hundred years later. Normally, reading was done aloud: the reader not only saw the words; he or she also heard them.

Reading, done aloud, slowly and even repetitively was closely linked with meditation. Meditation was a savoring of the text, a lingering on it, a total immersion in it. It involved memory as much as reflection. For medieval monks meditation meant hearing the text and learning it by heart. "Learning by heart" involves repeating a text over and over with ever-deeper understanding. When I learn by heart, I move the words from my mind into my heart, i.e., I "know" it with my heart as well as with my mind. I appropriate the words and make them my own. The texts belong to me. They constitute an important part of my mental and spiritual equipment. Yet they are not there just to be there. Their purpose is achieved only when they become principles of action, sources of motivation in my life. They help shape my inner psychology and my outward behavior. They are intended to move us to prayer and to action and even, when God chooses, to contemplation. Our task is to recognize the invitation to grow that they extend.

There is a big difference between "learning by heart" and "learning by rote." "Learning by rote" — a practice well known to Roman Catholics who as children spent hours struggling to "master" the catechism — is a process of committing an accumulation of words to memory with little attention to, and even less comprehension of, what the words really say. In some people memory can serve as a substitute for comprehension. I once had a student in class who had a phenomenal memory, but seemed to lack the powers of comprehension to match this remarkable gift. After one examination, I called her to my office and accused her of copying from the textbook. For she had reproduced parts of the textbook in response to each question on the test. The problem was that these answers, verbatim from the textbook, had nothing to do with the questions she was supposed to be answering. She insisted that she had not copied the answers and confidently asserted that she knew the entire text of the book word for word. And she did! One could ask her to start on any page and she could recite the text as long as you wished to listen. She had memorized the whole textbook, but apparently without expending much effort to understand what she had memorized.

It is important, then, to understand clearly that "learning by heart," to Anselm and his contemporaries, meant more than retaining "sounds." It meant seeing the text, hearing it, chewing it, and fixing it in memory in a reflective and understanding way. "Learning by heart" demanded involvement of the whole person and was oriented toward heart-felt prayer and, ultimately, toward genuine Christian living.

Living in an age in which we are deluged by information in a way unprecedented in human history, we tend to be memory-lazy. Why bother to "learn things by heart"? We have books, our own personal books and huge libraries, where we can easily look up whatever we want to know. We have the Internet and the world wide web to flood our minds with all sorts of information. We deal day after day with so many pieces of news, it is difficult for us to avoid living with unconnected bits of information and an unsorted mix of all sorts of knowledge. So much of what we see and hear remains at the surface of our minds. In such a situation, it is difficult for us to identify what is important, what we ought to be moving into our hearts. Yet it is what we fix in our hearts that enables us to become (or hinders us from becoming) the authentic persons we seek to be.

The monastic practice of *lectio divina*, engaging the mind, the memory, and the heart, can help us get our lives together. With time given regularly to this practice, our lives will cease, to some degree at least, being a jumble of events linked only by sequence of time and not by meaning. We will be better able to see where we are going in life and why. We will discover purpose and direction.

The important role that *lectio* played in the life of the monastery explains why monks had to be literate and why those who came to the monastery as young children had to be taught to read and write. The Rule of St. Benedict makes clear the prominent place of reading in the life of monks. Rule 48 says: "Idleness is the enemy of the soul. Therefore the brothers should have specified periods for manual labor as well as for prayerful reading [*lectio divina*]." Special importance was given to *lectio* during Lent. The same Rule 48 provides that at the beginning of Lent each monk "is to receive a book from the library and is to read the whole of it straight through." The intent of the reading was to stretch the mind and heart and thus direct the monk toward that single-minded search for God that defines Benedictine spirituality. So important was this reading in Benedict's Rule that he directed that two senior monks be appointed to make the rounds of the monastery to assure that no monk is "so apathetic as to waste time or engage in idle talk to the neglect of his reading."

The special importance given to Lenten reading simply highlights the fact that reading and meditation were a part of the daily schedule of the life of the monastery. This was particularly true for the Lord's Day. On Sunday all are to be engaged in reading except those who have been assigned various duties. If they are so remiss and indolent that they are unwilling or unable to study or to read, they are to be given some work in order that they may not be idle (Rule 48). It is worth pointing out that "to study or to read" is, in the Latin text, "meditare aut legere ("to meditate or read"). The intertwining of reading (seeing and hearing the word) and meditating (chewing, digesting the word that is read) is so close that the words are practically interchangeable.

Reading and meditating, it is important to emphasize, are engaged in not as ends in themselves (it's not a matter of just loading up the memory), but as proddings for prayer and conversion of life. They are elements of that search for simplicity of life and spiritual wholeness that are so essential to the monastic search for God — and, I would add, for anyone's authentic search for God.

Lectio divina (including reading, meditating, and praying) offers an important context for appreciating the role of prayer in Anselm's life. There is yet one other aspect of monastic life that also exercised a significant influence on his spirituality, namely, the liturgical worship of the monastery. As a monk Anselm was bound to the daily recitation of the Benedictine Office. As an ordained priest he would have celebrated the Eucharist, at least on

Sundays and important feast days. The language of the liturgy, especially the psalms, would have become a part of his thinking and praying vocabulary. Phrases from Scripture are easily identifiable in the prayers he wrote.

Anselm's Advice on Prayer

What if Anselm had written a book about prayer? What would he have said? What advice would he have given? Drawing on the few places where he does speak about how to pray, I want to attempt, in a brief way, to suggest the kind of advice he might have given. It would have been, I think, brief and simple. I offer just five points that, it seems to me, can be discovered in his prayers and in other places in his writings. I don't propose these as in any way definitive, but simply as points that have helped me and that may be helpful to the reader, as we make our way through Anselm's writings. These, I believe, are the issues he might have written about: (1) the attitude we must bring to prayer, (2) the "place" of prayer, (3) the proper use of prayer texts, (4) the climate of prayer, and (5) contemplation: the ultimate goal of the Christian journey. I shall discuss each of these in some detail.

The Attitude We Must Bring to Prayer

Anselm wants us to take our time with prayer. It is helpful, in beginning to pray, that we be quiet for a brief while in order to empty our minds of what might distract us in prayer. Anselm is very clear about the way we ought to pray: not quickly, but slowly. If we are praying with the Scriptures or with one of Anselm's prayers, we must be careful not to read them in the way we are accustomed to read the morning paper, that is, just skimming its contents and with only half-attention. In fact, the bad reading habits we unwittingly acquire in other types of daily reading may establish a pattern that becomes difficult to break when we come to pray. Speed-reading is the enemy of good prayer. One can no more pray in a hurry than make friends in a hurry or grow flowers in a hurry. Anselm is clear that what is being read is "not to be read casually or hurriedly, but a little at a time, with attentive care and thoughtful meditation" (S. III, 4). Nor should we set out to read as much as we can of the text we are using. Read only what is needed to stir up our spirit to pray. In fact it isn't even necessary, he tells us, to start at the beginning. We can start at any place in the reading that suits our fancy. Once again hear Anselm:

> The reader should strive to read
> not the whole of [the text],
> but only as much as, by God's help,
> will arouse the desire to pray,
> or bring enjoyment to the spirit.
> Nor is there any need to start always at the beginning.
> [It suffices to begin] wherever one finds it pleasing to do so.
>
> (S. III, 3)

The important thing is to find and ponder deeply whatever makes us *want* to pray. Our hearts may be tightly closed: prayer stretches them and makes them capable of loving God. Our minds may be so cluttered with troublesome distractions that there is no room for prayer. You cannot put water into a glass that is already filled to the brim. Anselm wants us, as far as we can, to let the prayer texts we use open our hearts and unclutter our minds. Then we can truly pray. Our prayer leads us to compunction, that piercing of our hearts that fills us with a sorrowing repentance for our sins and with a deep longing for God. Compunction of heart tells us two things: (1) we are wretched sinners undeserving of God's love, (2) we are the image of God and the object of God's loving and unconditional concern.

The "Place" of Prayer

In the *Proslogion,* a book that is about God and written in the form of a prayer to God, Anselm deals with the inner disposition we must bring to prayer if we hope to pray well. At the beginning of the *Proslogion* he addresses himself (though he would want to include the reader as well) in these words:

> Come now, insignificant person,
> flee for a while your usual occupations,
> hide yourself for a time from disturbing thoughts,
> cast aside for now burdensome cares,
> free yourself a little for God
> and rest a while in God.
> Enter the inner room of your mind,
> shut out everything except God
> and whatever may help you in your search for God.
> Close the door and seek God.
> Speak now, my whole heart,
> speak to God: "I seek your face,
> O Lord, your face, I seek." (S. I, 97)

Anyone who is serious about growing spiritually can easily identify with Anselm's call "to get away from it all" for a while so that we can collect our wits, get our heads on straight, and make sure we are moving in the right direction. Inner silence is most important: we must strive to empty our minds and still our hearts; yet this inner disposition of spirit is difficult to achieve without some amount of external quiet and solitude.

Recently I read about a professor at Cambridge who invited a student to his home. The student asked him why he had named his home Zoar. The professor answered: "Read the nineteenth chapter of Genesis and you will understand." If you check that chapter you will find that it tells the story of Lot fleeing from the burning city of Sodom. God speaks to him and tells him to take refuge in the hill country. Lot had no desire to start a new life in the barren Judean hills. He begged God to let him go to a quiet little city nearby. The city was named Zoar. God gave him permission. The professor told his student: "Whenever things get too hot at the university, I give myself permission to retire for a while to Zoar."

Anselm, especially after he became archbishop of Canterbury, would have readily identified with the professor's strategy for dealing with life's turmoil and stress. We all need a "Zoar" in our lives. It's wonderful if Zoar can be a place, but often it can't. In its deepest sense, Zoar is a dimension of the human spirit. It's resting a while in God. It's closing the door of our minds for a while so that afterward we can open them to the cares and concerns that must necessarily be part of our lives. We go aside not to escape people, but to get a true perspective on life so that we can deal with people gently, caringly, and lovingly. We seek the face of God in prayer so that we may have the wisdom that sees the face of God in our sisters and brothers.

The Proper Use of Prayer Texts

If we use Scripture texts or formulated prayers (like the ones Anselm composed), we should open our minds and hearts so that these texts may stir us to genuine prayer of our own. Anselm, in sending a copy of his prayers to the Countess Matilda, indicated to her that "they are arranged so that by reading them, the mind may be stirred either to love or fear of God or to a consideration of both." In other words, the texts we use are tools. They are intended to be proddings to our hearts. They are not goals, but means leading us to prayer, stimulating us to compunction and spiritual growth.

Readers who know Zen Buddhism will recall the apparently outrageous advice that the Zen masters give to their students: "Burn the Scriptures!" It isn't that the Zen masters have no respect for the Buddhist Scriptures. But they want their students to learn that just reading, without letting the reading do something to them, will never lead them to enlightenment. The same basic message is clear in a charming Jewish story about the young student who came to his rabbi and asked what he must do to achieve eternal life. The rabbi asked him what had he already done. With some pride the student replied: "I have gone through the entire Torah." "Ah," the rabbi said: "But has the Torah gone through you?" Prayer is a way in which we let the Word of God penetrate us through and through, to deepen our closeness to God and our concern for God's people.

The Climate of Prayer: Dealing with Turmoil

Anselm wants us to come to prayer with our hearts quiet, relaxed, reflective. Thus he writes in the preface to his book of prayers: The prayers "are not to be read in turmoil, but quietly." In what I have already quoted from the *Proslogion* the same point is made: "Flee [he tells us] from your usual occupations, hide yourself from disturbing thoughts, cast aside for now burdensome cares." We may be inclined to say: "Father Abbot, that's a great ideal you're proposing to us. How wonderful it would be if we could pray with quiet, relaxed, reflective hearts. Maybe that can happen in a monastery. But we don't live in monasteries. For the vast majority of us it's not often that life puts us in this ideal situation for prayer. All too frequently we find that we have to bring the turmoil and frustrations of our lives to prayer or we wouldn't be praying at all."

Anselm, I think, would have sympathized with this problem more after he became archbishop than when he had been abbot. As archbishop he found that all too often he had to be away from his monastery and was forced to deal with problems that engendered turmoil and disquiet in his own life. According to the Rule of St. Benedict, monks, when away from their monastery, "are not to omit the prescribed hours but to observe them as best they can" (chapter 50). We have every reason to believe that as a deeply committed monk Anselm would have been careful to observe this rule. He would have continued his prayer-life, no matter where he was or how unlikely for prayer his situation might have been. In this context he might well have thought of chapter 68 of the Rule, which deals with a situation where a monk is assigned a task that he feels is impossible for him to do. The Rule says, in effect: if the abbot insists, then do it anyway. Now, of course, Anselm was the abbot, but we know that as abbot he was stricter with himself than with the monks bound in obedience to him. It is fair, then, to think that he would have taken chapter 68 of the Rule most seriously. In discussing this chapter of the Rule, Joan Chittister quotes a wise Jewish proverb: "when you have no choice, don't be afraid."[1]

If we truly wish to experience God in our lives, we have no choice. We must find some place, some time, where, despite the inevitable turmoil that life brings, we can be silently and quietly with God. It may seem like the impossible dream. Yet we must not forget that, when we strive to do what seems impossible to us, we are not left alone and simply on our own resources. The

---

1. Chittister, *The Rule of St. Benedict,* 173.

God whom we seek in prayer is the God who is seeking us. This God is the God who spoke to Moses, gave him what seemed to be an impossible task, and then simply told him: "Don't be afraid. I shall be with you." It may be that it is precisely in the midst of turmoil and anguish that we discover God doing in us what we can't do by ourselves: namely, leading us into an atmosphere of peace and quiet. After all, in its most radical meaning, prayer is an expression of our deepest realization that we are totally dependent on God. Without God we can do nothing. Without God we are nothing. The best prayer is not necessarily the comfortable prayer nor is it necessarily the one in which we are the least distracted. The best prayer is the one that puts us in touch with our own createdness and our need for God. It's the prayer in which we experience ourselves as nothing and God as all. This is an experience of peace and quiet, no matter what storms may be swirling about us.

Perhaps we all need to return often to these words of Anselm, calling us "to hide for a time from disturbing thoughts and cast aside burdensome cares." We need to seek solitude and silence or at least whatever silence and solitude we can manage. Yet withal we have to face the reality of our own life situation. The work we do may be demanding. The relationships we have to deal with may be draining. Our schedule of necessary activities may be exhausting. It is in such a context — our real world — that we must search for silence and solitude. Honesty in the search may force us to do some rethinking of our priorities.

Contemplation: The Ultimate Goal of the Christian Journey

There is a brief section of the prayer that begins the *Proslogion* which sums up the spiritual journey as Anselm sees it:

> Teach me to seek you
> and show yourself to me as I seek;
> for I am not able to seek you unless you teach me;
> nor am I able to find you unless you show me [the way].
> Let me seek you in desiring you,

and desire you in seeking you.
May I find you in loving you,
and love you in finding you. (S. I, 100)

Note the verbs in this brief bit of prayer. They may be read as something of a summary of the essential elements of Anselm's spirituality: the way of progressing in that spirituality and the goal to which it is intended to lead us. We ask God to "teach" us: spirituality is not something we can achieve simply by our own efforts. We need to be taught by God and led by God's grace. The other verbs specify what we need to be taught.

One of the verbs is *desire:* the desires of our hearts must be purified. Alan Jones, in his book on Dante, *The Soul's Journey,* suggests that the theme of Dante's great poem is the purification of desires. This "purification of desires" is what Anselm and the Rule of St. Benedict meant by "compunction." Our desires have to be educated: we have to learn what is worthy of our desiring. This means learning that our desiring will never come to an end until it finds its place of rest in God. We move from the "compunction of tears" to the "compunction of the heart" yearning for God. In the concluding lines of the *Paradiso* the poet finds desire's rest in "the Love that moves the sun and all the stars."

Desire leads to *seeking.* Seeking God gives a direction to our lives, a sense of where we want to go. Eventually it brings me the realization that the God whom I seek is the God who, ever so much more ardently, seeks me. I become aware, too, that the God I seek is not somewhere outside of me; God is within me. As M. B. Pranger has written in an article comparing St. Anselm and St. Bernard: "God who is the ultimate object of desire, not only governs the process of the human quest for himself, but he is also involved and present in that process all along."[2] Yet at times we seem to flee from God, as Francis Thompson writes in his poem *The Hound of Heaven* (a poem, incidentally, that I think Anselm would have admired):

---

2. *Anselm: Aosta, Bec, and Canterbury,* 136.

> I fled Him, down the nights and down the days;
> I fled Him, down the arches of the years;
> I fled Him, down the labyrinthine ways
> Of my own mind; and in the midst of tears
> I hid from Him.

Sometimes we appear to hide because we have our hearts set on other things, and we fear that seeking God may cut us off from what we think our hearts desire. To quote Thompson again: "Yet was I sore adread lest having Him, I must have naught beside." Yet, even as we may seem to seek escape from its longing embrace, God's grace continues to draw us to conversion, to change, to gradual transformation, to a deeper spirituality. The "Hound of Heaven" never ceases from the pursuit:

> Ah, fondest, blindest, weakest,
> I am He Whom thou seekest!
> Thou dravest love from thee, who dravest Me.

Thus it is that seeking leads to *loving*. Again the "Hound of Heaven":

> Whom wilt thou find to love ignoble thee,
> Save Me, save only Me?

God loves us! And it is because God loves us that we are able to love. In John's first epistle, we read: "We love [i.e., are able to love], because God loved us" (1 John 4:19). We discover that in loving God, we learn to love all God's creatures: not in a grasping or possessive way, but in a caring and wholesome way that enables us to see and appreciate God's image in all that God has made. Indeed, we come to realize that they and we are all one in God.

And, at last, loving leads to *finding*. Finding fulfills love's yearnings. For it means loving in an absolute way. It is in finding God, in the totality of our lives (with all that finding God means in terms of the proper ordering of our lives), that the goal of the spiritual journey is achieved. Pedro Arrupe, former superior general of the Jesuits, has expressed so clearly and in so practical a way what it means to find God:

> Nothing is more practical than finding God, than falling in love in a quite absolute, final way. What you are in love with will affect everything. It will decide what will get you out of bed in the morning, what you will do with your evenings, how you spend your weekends, what you read, who you know, what breaks your heart, and what amazes you with joy and gratitude.
>
> Finding God is but another word for the goal of a contemplative spirituality.[3]

It was toward this *finding* that Anselm's spirituality kept leading him. It is toward this finding of God within us and in all of reality that all our lives are directed.

For one who lives a contemplative spirituality, contemplation is the highest reach of prayer. It is God's gift of a total awareness of God. At this point, we put aside texts and words, images and concepts, as we enter into God's silence and God's love, and experience, in so far as we can in this life, our oneness with God. We come to realize that God alone truly exists and that everything else exists only in God and because God loves it and sustains it. The only experience that lies beyond is the beatific vision.

An Example of a Prayer Experience Using One of Anselm's Prayers

I have suggested five bits of advice that I think might constitute a brief Anselmian approach to prayer and have tried to clarify what I mean by them. Anselm might well have reacted

---

3. Strangely, these words of Father Arrupe have been quoted many times, but no one seems to know when or where he spoke them. Father Vincent O'Keefe, who was closely associated with him, writes that he searched Father Arrupe's writings, but was unable to locate the source of these remarks. His conclusion is that Father Arrupe spoke these words to some group. The words were recorded by someone who heard them, but were never put in writing by him.

to such advice in something of this fashion: "Yes, I suppose what you have written could be helpful and does more or less represent what I might say. But don't ask people to worry too much about theories of prayer. Just tell them to go ahead. Invite them to pray." Assuming this reaction from him (which perhaps is a bit presumptuous of me), I want to offer an example of an Anselmian prayer experience, making use of the prayer that is part of the first chapter of the *Proslogion*. I invite you, the reader, to read this prayer slowly and reflectively, pausing when it moves you to prayer of your own. Before presenting the prayer, I want offer a brief introduction to it.

The goal of this powerful prayer is stated immediately. Anselm begs for what is a constant theme in the psalms: to see God face to face, or, put more paradoxically, to see the face of One who has no face. The prayer expresses the deepest problem that faith must address: the inaccessibility of a God who yet is everywhere. He prays that God may give him a sign whereby he can properly search for God. It is not clear what sign he means. Perhaps it is the moment of enlightenment he will speak about in the famous chapter 2 of the *Proslogion* (which we shall discuss later). The prayer begins with a plea for instruction, not just for the mind but for the heart:

> Now then, O Lord my God, teach my heart:
> where and how to seek you,
> where and how to find you.
> Lord, if you are not here,
> where am I to seek you in your absence?
> Yet if you are everywhere,
> why do I not see you in your presence?
> (S. I, 98)

This is the paradox that Anselm is often puzzling over: why is it that, if God is everywhere, I cannot see him? It is the question that has engaged thinkers through the ages. It is at the heart of the "problem of God." Anselm continues.

> Of course, you dwell in light inaccessible.
> And where is that light inaccessible?

> And who will lead me and bring me to it,
> so that in it I may see you?
> And then by what signs and in what form
> shall I seek you?
> Never have I seen you, O Lord, my God.
> I do not know your face.

At this point in the prayer Anselm, still speaking to God, moves to the third person, as he is about to talk, not just about his own plight, but about the general condition of humanity after the fall. His prayer becomes the prayer of every man, every woman, living in exile from their true homeland (I should point out that Anselm, living long before an age of language inclusivism, follows the custom of his time in using the male pronoun for any human person). Almost mantra-like the prayer struggles for different ways to articulate the anguish of separation from God and the longing to find God and to experience God. It is a fundamental human hunger that he expresses: the deep human frustration experienced in being created for God and yet unable to achieve creation's goal. More positively, Anselm's words may be read as a kind of reprise on the words of St. Augustine: "Our hearts are restless, till they find their rest in you."

> What shall he do, O highest Lord,
> what shall he do, this exile, so long a time away from you?
> What shall your servant do,
> yearning for your love, yet cast so far away from your face?
> He yearns to see you,
> but your face is so far away from him.
> He desires to come to you,
> but your dwelling-place is inaccessible.
> He wants to find you,
> yet knows not where you are.
> He yearns to seek you,
> but does not recognize your face.

Note the verbs that Anselm uses here: "desiring," "seeking," "yearning," "finding." Earlier in discussing Anselm's prayer

advice, I quoted similar verbs from the *Proslogion.* Anselm
continues:

> O Lord, you are my God, you are my Lord.
> Yet I have never seen you.
> You have created me and recreated me,
> you have given me all the good things I have,
> and still I do not know you.
> I was made to see you, and I have not yet achieved
> that for which I was made.

The prayer continues with a description of the sorry state
of humanity as a result of Adam's sin. There is something of
the lament: "if only he had not. . . ." There is the mystery of
the appalling contrast between the original blessing God gave
to humankind and the present state in which humanity finds
itself. In vivid metaphors Anselm sets what *might have been*
against what *actually is.* Each metaphor calls for reflection on
the human condition with which all of us can easily identify.

At one point he seems to reprimand Adam for not keeping
for us what he could easily have kept and what we find so difficult to recover. I am reminded of a cartoon in *Commonweal* that
shows God pointing an accusing finger at the forlorn couple,
Adam and Eve, as they stand beneath a fruit tree. Adam, hold-
ing a half-eaten apple in his hand, pleads: "We couldn't help
it. We had no role models." The sad human story is that they
themselves became weak and frail models for a fallen humanity.

> O sorry lot of humanity
> that has lost that for which it was made!
> O hard and terrible that fall.
> Alas, what was lost and what was found!
> What is gone and what remains!
> Humans lost the happiness for which they were made
> and found the misery for which they were not made.
> Then they ate the bread of angels for which now they
>   hunger.
> Now they eat the bread of sorrows which then they did not
>   know.

Alas, the common grief of humankind,
the universal lament of Adam's children.
He was filled to satiety; we sigh in hunger.
He possessed in abundance; we are forced to beg.
What he possessed in happiness, he unhappily lost.
What we so unhappily lack, we long for in our misery,
But, alas, we remain empty.
Why did he not keep for us,
when he could so easily have done so,
what we now so grievously lack?
Why did he turn the light off for us,
even draw the darkness over us,
why take life from us and afflict us with death?
Wretched creatures that we are,
whence have we been expelled,
to where are we being driven,
whence cast out, to what depths have we sunk?
From our homeland into exile
from the vision of God into the blindness that is ours,
from the joy of immortality into the bitterness and horror of
    death.
What a miserable exchange!
From such great good into such great evil.
How grave our loss, how grievous our sorrow,
wholly to be lamented.

Then from the fallen state of all humanity, Anselm returns
to his own personal sorry state: what he desires most ardently
he seems unable to achieve. Every facet of human estrangement
from God is prayerfully, almost agonizingly, scrutinized. At the
same time, like Jacob, he wrestles with God; like Job, he asks for
answers.

O, alas, wretch that I am,
one of Eve's children, separated from God.
What have I undertaken and what have I actually achieved?
Where am I going, what have I come to?
To what am I aspiring,
for what do I yearn?

I sought your goodness and, behold, confusion.
I was moving toward God and I got in my own way.
I sought peace within me,
and found only tribulation and sorrow in my inmost self.
I wanted to smile out of the joy in my mind,
and I am compelled to frown because of the sorrow in my
    heart.
I longed for joy, yet my sighs kept increasing.
And you, O Lord, how long
how long, O Lord, will you forget us,
how long will you turn your face away from us?
When will you look on us and hear us,
when will you give light to our eyes and show us your face?
When will you restore yourself to us?

In a bold touch we are hardly prepared for, Anselm has, in the last few verses above, chided God in a series of questions that almost take on the character of a demand, even a reprimand: "How long will you turn your face away?" "When will you restore yourself to us?" The impatience, buried in these words, seems almost to call God to account. The genuineness of this petulant questioning of God gives the prayer a ring of honesty and authenticity.

I am reminded of the rabbi who came upon the town tailor who was swaying and groaning and mumbling in prayer. "What has happened?" the rabbi asked. The tailor answered: "Rabbi, I was arguing with God. I'm not a good man," he continued. "I have charged customers more than I have a right to. I have often done sloppy work. But I'm not really bad either. But look at the way God behaves and how difficult God makes our lives. So I bargained. I told God I would forgive all the sins God committed against me, if God would forgive me mine. Was that wrong, rabbi?" "Not at all," the rabbi answered, "but why did you let God off so lightly?" The rabbi's words call to mind the so-called "confessions" of Jeremiah, where he chides God for having unfairly enticed him into his most unhappy role as a prophet:

You duped me, O Lord, and I let myself be duped;
You were too strong for me, and you triumphed. . . .
The word of the Lord
has brought me derision and reproach all the day.

(Jer. 20:7–8)

Thus far Anselm's prayer has presented a grim picture of human wretchedness. We are moved to inquire: Are things really that bad? Anselm would be inclined to say: yes. At the same time he would make clear that the Christian message is always one of hope. What we cannot do, God can do for us. God can give us illumination and strength. We approach in poverty, but to the One who is all-rich. We come in misery, but to One who is Compassion. When we are stooped over and unable by our own efforts even to look up in God's direction, God lifts us up toward divinity. God teaches us to do what we cannot do alone. God enables us to believe. God enables us to understand what we believe. One is reminded of the hopeful optimism of St. Paul: "Where sin increased, grace abounded all the more" (Rom. 5:20). Notice how this section of the prayer begins in the first person plural and then moves to the singular:

Look, Lord, hear us, enlighten us, show us yourself.
That it may go well with us, restore to us your very self
without whom it will go ill with us.
Have mercy on our labors, our efforts to reach you,
for without you what we do is without avail.
You call us. So help us!
I beg, Lord, that I may not sigh in despair,
but rather draw my breath in hope,
that, though my heart is embittered with desolation,
you will sweeten it with consolation.
I beg, Lord, that hungering for you, I may seek you,
and thus give up my fasting for you.
In poverty I have come to one who is rich,
in misery to one who is compassion.
Now if I sigh before I eat, let me eat after my sighing.

Stooped over as I am, I can only look down,
lift me that my gaze may be directed upward.
My transgressions pour over my head,
cover me like a heavy burden, weigh me down,
free me, unburden me,
lest the pit of iniquity close its mouth over me.
Let me look toward your light,
whether from afar or from the depths.
Teach me to seek you and show yourself to me as I seek,
for I cannot seek you unless you teach me,
or find you unless you show me where you are.
May I seek you by desiring you
and desire you in seeking you.
May I find you by loving you
and love you in finding you.
I acknowledge you, Lord, and give you thanks,
because you have created me in your image,
that remembering you, I may think of you
and thinking of you love you.
But that image has been disfigured by a multitude of vices,
and darkened by the smoke of sin,
so that it cannot do what it was made to do,
unless you renew and reform it.
I do not attempt, Lord, to attain your lofty heights,
since my mind is not equal to the task.
But I desire in some measure to understand your truth,
which my heart believes and loves.
For I do not seek to understand in order to believe,
rather I believe in order that I may understand.
This also I believe:
that unless I believe,
I shall not understand. (S. I, 98–99)

These final lines of this moving prayer present briefly Anselm's approach to faith. This is most important in understanding his life's journey to God. We shall be discussing in
detail in the next chapter the precise meaning that faith had
for him.

The Prayers and Meditations

Though Anselm never wrote a formal treatise on prayer, one of his earliest writings was a book of prayers and meditations. As a book of prayers and reflections for individuals, it was so unique that R. W. Southern has called it the "Anselmian revolution." A form of devotional writing, intended for individual rather than community prayer, these prayers and meditations enjoyed an immense popularity in the later Middle Ages. If imitation is the highest form of flattery, Anselm was highly flattered indeed: many imitations of his prayers came to be included with the genuine ones. The tangled mix was sorted out only in the early twentieth century when Dom A. Wilmart identified the handful (but how wonderful a handful) of authentic prayers of Anselm among hundreds of aliens. In the Schmitt edition there are nineteen prayers and three meditations.

The prayers seemed to have achieved a good bit of popularity in Anselm's day also. Otto Pacht, in an article entitled "The Illustrations of St. Anselm's Prayers and Meditations," includes a number of interesting pictorial miniatures that were used to illustrate the *Prayers and Meditations*.[4] Pacht suggests that the pictorial illustration may have been produced during Anselm's lifetime, perhaps even at his own instigation. One shows Anselm handing out scrolls to a group of monks on either side of him. A second pictures the enthroned archbishop handing the manuscript to the Countess Matilda. In yet another he and Matilda are seen worshipping together the vision of Christ in majesty.

At the time Anselm wrote his *Prayers and Meditations*, a form of devotional writing for the laity already existed, but it was largely made up of verses from the psalms, sometimes with short reflections attached. The prayers and meditations became with Anselm a new form of religious literature. They are the most monastic of his writings. And it may confidently be said that they grew out of his own personal prayer, as his spirituality was fed by the daily exercises of reading, meditation, prayer and liturgy in the monastery. They can hardly be described,

---

4. *Journal of the Warburg and Courtauld Institutes* 19 (1956): 71.

however, as spontaneous outpourings of the human spirit. In the form in which they have come down to us, they are carefully crafted works that at their best are writings of impressive literary beauty. R. W. Southern has pointed out Anselm's "talent for coining phrases which astonish the reader by their boldness."[5] There is a frequent play on words as well as a playing with words. Verbal antitheses repeatedly occur. Thus, to take a simple example, in the Prayer to God (no. 1) we read: "Semper, Domine, ad meliora cum humilitate proficere et numquam deficere." Note the antitheses: *semper* (always) and *numquam* (never), *proficere* (to advance) and *deficere* (to go backward, to fail, to fall short). Sister Benedicta Ward's translation — "Always, Lord, let me go with humility to better things and never grow slack" — conveys the sense of the text, but not its carefully balanced rhetoric. An attempt at a literal translation: "Let me with humility always advance toward better things and never go backward in doing so" is no better; in fact it is clumsy and doesn't really convey the antitheses any more than Ward's more literate rendering of the text. There is artistry, sometimes bordering on artificiality and overload, in the Latin texts of Anselm's writings that simply cannot be conveyed in a translation. Anyone who has ever attempted to translate knows that there is never a completely satisfactory way of putting one language into another. But even in translation Anselm's prayers and meditations, I am convinced, will be able to accomplish the purpose he intended: namely, to stir the thoughtful reader to prayer.

The prayers and meditations were initially put together at the request of some of his brother monks at Bec. One might ask the question: should prayers be as carefully crafted (as I have suggested these are), unless perhaps they are intended for public use (and even there it should not be overdone)? Does this not make for a certain formality in a form of prayer that ought to be spontaneous and relaxed? Perhaps the appropriate way to respond to these questions is simply to point out what I have already suggested, namely, that Anselm's intent in writing these prayers was not that they be recited as prayers, but instead that they be used to stir the reader to genuine prayer of his or her

---

5. *St. Anselm: A Portrait in a Landscape*, 108.

own. He does not so much invite us to make his prayers ours as to use his to stimulate our own. He wants them to prod the reader's spirit. As he wrote in the preface to them: "The purpose of the prayers and meditations is to stir up the mind of the reader to the love or fear of God or to self-examination." The term "self-examination" as a goal for the reader gives us an insight into what is a basic element of these prayers: the self-naughting, the self-accusation, the lengthy confession of sins that may at times seem a bit overdone to twentieth-century men and women. Still we must not miss the fact (by no means absent from these prayers) that this ascetical dimension of our lives is not something to be sought for its own sake; rather it is intended to lead us to prayer and ultimately to contemplation.

Most of the prayers are addressed to particular saints: St. Mary, St. John the Baptist, St. Peter, St. Paul, St. John the Evangelist, St. Stephen, St. Nicholas, St. Benedict, St. Mary Magdalene. The prayers to the saints are lively, deeply personal conversations with them, as these special friends of God are addressed as immediately and intimately present. They celebrate, in other words, that wondrous union between earth and heaven which we call the communion of saints. There is a thin veil — thinner perhaps than we realize — between this world and those who have attained the fullness of God. Anselm would have appreciated the thoughts of Zozima the Elder in Dostoevsky's novel *The Brothers Karamazov:* "Much on earth is concealed from us, but in place of it we have been granted a secret, mysterious sense of our living bonds with the other world, with the higher heavenly world.... "

The prayers are highly introspective. They dwell, as I have already said, on the sinfulness of the one who prays as a necessary step to conversion. At the same time the saint is not always spared. The sinfulness in their earthly existence of those who have achieved life's final goal offers the sinner who prays a source of comfort and a point of kinship with the saints. Though now fully redeemed and enjoying the vision of God, they too were once sinners, as truly as the one who now prays. While their sinfulness is noted, at the same time their virtues and privileges are praised. All this leads to prayers asking for their intercession.

Prayer to St. Peter

The Prayer to St. Peter may serve as an example. Anselm praises the gifts of Peter:

Holy and most kind Peter,
faithful shepherd of God's sheep,
prince of the Apostles,
prince among such great princes,
you bind and loose what you will,
you heal and bring to life whom you will,
you give the kingdom of heaven to whom you will.
O great Peter, you are great indeed,
for you are endowed with so many and such great gifts,
you have been elevated to so many and such great dignities.

This calling upon St. Peter and naming his greatness is followed by Anselm's cry for the saint's intercession:

Behold me, the poorest and weakest of men,
surrounded by many serious difficulties and hardships.
In my misery I need the help of your kind power,
but my mouth lacks the words to express what I really need.
My heart lacks the fervor that I would need
to rise from my lowliness to your lofty heights....
Alas, I am the most wretched of wretches.
This is really so. I am not pretending.

Anselm describes himself as a sickly sheep groaning at the shepherd's feet, seeking access to Peter the shepherd. Suddenly, in the midst of his protestation of his own wretchedness and his need for the prayers of the one whom Christ made shepherd of the sheep, he rather slyly inserts at least one point of contrast between himself (now spoken of in the third person) and Peter:

He may have made his mistakes,
but at least he did not deny his Lord and Shepherd.

(S. III, 30–33)

Prayers to Mary

Perhaps the most remarkable of the prayers are those to St. Mary. At first they posed a problem to his methodology. Mary was uniquely different from the other saints. They were sinners like Anselm himself, but Mary was sinless. How could Anselm the sinner identify with the sinless one? Besides, there was little in Scripture of inspired phrases extolling her. He struggled with the problem of how to pray to her, writing three versions before he was satisfied. In the second version he used a bold phrase *mundi reconciliatrix* (reconciliatrix of the world). It was a phrase to which he never again returned, probably because it implied more than he wanted to say. For he believed that it was Christ alone who reconciled the world to God. The methodology he finally hit upon was to stress, with a torrent of descriptive phrases, the exaltation of Mary in Christ's redeeming act.[6]

This third prayer begins with words of praise for Mary: "the great Mary, the most blessed of all Marys, the greatest of all women." His whole being wants to praise her: his heart to love her, his mouth to sing her praises, his mind to venerate her, his soul to pray to her with loving affection. For she is "queen of the angels, Lady of the world, mother of him who saved the world." Words fail him as he tries to say what is worthy of her.

> What can I say that is worthy of the Mother of my creator
>   and my savior?
> For [it is] by her holiness that my sins are taken away,
> by her uprightness that I gain immortality....
> By her fruitfulness that I have been redeemed from my
>   captivity,
> by her child-bearing that I have been saved from eternal
>   death,

---

6. Speaking of the third of these prayers, Anselm writes to Gundulf, a monk at Canterbury, that a brother had asked him to write a prayer to Mary. He wrote one, then another, and was satisfied with neither. Finally he wrote a third which, he says, "seems satisfactory for the moment" (Letter 28, *Letters*, 1:121). Speaking of this third prayer, which represents Anselm's most mature reflection on Mary, Benedicta Ward writes: "It is a cosmic view of redemption in which, as in an icon, Christ is the central figure and Mary shows him to us and us to him" (*The Prayers and Meditations of St. Anselm*, 63–64).

through her child that I who once was lost
have been restored [to life],
rescued from hapless exile
and brought back to the blessed homeland.

Though he claims to be lost for words he continues to pile up terms of praise and honor for Mary. One of the highlights of the prayer is a jubilant paean to her glory.

O thing of wonder!
At what sublime heights do I look when I look at Mary!
Nothing is equal to Mary,
nothing save God is greater than Mary....
All nature is created by God.
And God is born of Mary!
God created all things,
Mary gave birth to God!
God made all things;
he made himself from Mary
and thus remade everything God had made.
God who can make all things from nothing
refused to remake it by doing it violence.
He chose instead to become son of Mary.
Therefore God is the creator of all things,
and Mary is the mother of all that is created anew.
God is the father who constitutes all things,
Mary the mother who reconstitutes all things.
God gave birth to the One through whom all things are
    made;
Mary brought forth the One through whom all are saved.
God gave birth to the One without whom nothing exists;
Mary brought forth the One without whom nothing is wholly
    good.
O truly the Lord is with you,
to whom the Lord gave
that all nature owes only to you
that it belongs with him.

In the following section, which concludes the prayer, he invokes Jesus, as he frequently does in these prayers, and then talks alternately with Jesus and Mary.

Surely Jesus, Son of God, and you, Mary his mother,
both want (and it is only right),
that whatever you love, should be loved by us also.
So good Son, I ask you through the love
by which you love your mother,
that as you truly love her and want her to be loved,
that you grant that I may truly love her.
Good Mother,
I ask you through the love
by which you love your son,
that as you truly love him and want him to be loved
you grant that I may truly love him.
For, look, I am asking for is surely what you want,
for why does he not do to me [what I deserve]
on account of my sins,
since it is in his power to do so?
Lover and Savior of humankind,
you were able to love even to death your accusers.
Could you possibly refuse to hear
the prayers of those who love you and your mother?
Mother of our lover who carried him in your womb
and nursed him at your breasts,
could it [ever happen] that you would be unable or unwilling
to grant your love and his to those who seek it?
So I venerate both of you,
as much as my mind is worthy to do so,
I love both of you
as much as my heart is equal to it;
I esteem both of you
as much as my soul is able.
And I serve both of you
as much as my flesh ought to do.
And may my life be fulfilled in this:
that for all eternity my whole being may sing,
"Blessed be the Lord forever. Amen." (S. III, 18–25)

Prayer to St. Paul

A significant characteristic of the prayers is the linking of the intercession of the saints with the mediation of Christ, the one mediator between God and us. Anselm never lost sight of the fundamental truth that, while the saints may help and encourage us on our pilgrim way, it is Christ alone who saves. This is expressed in a striking way in the Prayer to St. Paul.

O Paul, where is he,
the one who was called the nurse of the faithful,
cherishing his children?
Where is that affectionate mother who proclaims everywhere
that she is once again in labor for her children?
Sweet nurse, sweet mother,
who are the children with whom you are in labor
or whom you are nursing,
but those whom you bring forth and instruct
by teaching them the faith of Christ?
And after you what Christian is there
who was not born and confirmed in the faith by your
  teaching?
So then, St. Paul, your son is this dead man.
Mother, this dead man is certainly your son.
Dear mother, recognize your son
in the voice of his confession.
May he recognize his mother in her compassionate love.

Later in the Prayer, Anselm addresses Jesus:

And you, Jesus, dear Lord, are you not also a mother?
Are you not a mother who, like a hen,
gathers her chickens under her wings?
Truly you are a mother....
In your desire to bring your children into life
you tasted of death,
and in your dying you gave them birth.
You did this of your own self;
others at your command and with your help.

You as author, they as ministers.
Therefore, O Lord God, you are mother most of all.

(S. III, 39–40)

Note the contrast between Jesus and his servants: he is the author of salvation, they are but the ministers. "You did this of your own self; others at your command and with your help." Daring and striking in this prayer is the beautiful image of Jesus as our mother. Many associate this image with Julian of Norwich, without realizing that it was used three centuries earlier by Anselm and that Julian was probably indebted to the abbot of Bec for this impressive and moving image of Jesus. Today, as we struggle to find terms for designating God and the Risen Jesus which are not gender-exclusive, it is helpful to know that Anselm, who can hardly be described as a feminist, was — centuries ago — offering a helpful approach to an issue that did not even exist in his day.

Prayer to St. John the Baptist

Another example of the contrast between the Lord who saves and the saint who is saved (and then able to help us on our way to salvation) may be found in the prayer to St. John the Baptist. Note the typical ascetical approach: Anselm begs for healing and reconciliation. Clearly it is the Lord alone who can heal him; the Baptist can only pray for that healing. Toward the end of the prayer we read:

True healer, I beg you, heal me;
true witness, I plead with you: pray for me.
Reconcile me to myself....
Let me experience what I hear and feel what I believe.
Jesus, gentle Lord, if you do what he says you do,
let it be done in me.
John, revealer of God, if you witness to what God has done,
let it be done in me according to your word.
Lord, source of healing, heal me.
Accomplish this in me, Lord, since you can do so.

You, Lord, are [simply] great,
and you, John, are "great in the sight of the Lord."

(S. III, 29)

The two final verses are straight from the Gospel according to
Luke, where the evangelist contrasts John, who is called "great
in the sight of God," with Jesus who is simply called "great" (a
common description of God in the Hebrew Scriptures).

Prayer to St. Mary Magdalene

I have suggested earlier the importance of compunction in Anselm's understanding of spirituality. It was not a term that
originated with him. The word can be traced back to the New
Testament. Peter preaches on Pentecost about the resurrection of
Jesus and the need for repentance to enable one to share in the
mystery of the Risen Jesus; and we are told that those who hear
him "were pierced to the heart" (*compuncti sunt corde*, Acts 2:17).
The Latin word *compungere* means "to pierce." In its profane
sense it refers to "any acute (physical) pain"; in the monastic
tradition, it is the spiritual pain experienced by our sense of sinfulness, but also the sense of our longing for God. The article in
the *New Catholic Encyclopedia* sums up four stages of compunction as described by St. Gregory in his *Moralia on the Book of Job*:
(1) being overcome with shame (a consciousness of where one
has been), (2) a realization of the just punishment due to sin (the
consciousness of where one *will be*), (3) a recognition of the per-
ilous situation in which a person finds himself or herself, where
sin still remains a possibility (a consciousness of where one actually *is*), and (4) an intense longing for the heavenly home (a
consciousness of where one *has not yet* arrived).

The Rule of St. Benedict draws heavily on Scripture and
Christian tradition. It can be expected, then, that compunction
will play an important role in the Rule. Rule 20, which is about
"Reverence in Prayer," says: "We must know that God regards
our purity of heart and tears of compunction, not our many
words." Rule 49, which deals with the "Observance of Lent,"
invites the monks to devote themselves "to prayer with tears,
to reading, to compunction of heart and self-denial." Anselm

would have been acquainted with the *Moralia* of St. Gregory, and of course he lived by the Rule of St. Benedict. Compunction is a key element in his understanding of spirituality.

With this fairly long introduction to the prayer to St. Mary Magdalene, I want to suggest that in this prayer Anselm prays for the gift of compunction. In accordance with the scriptural understanding of his day, he identifies Magdalene with the sinful woman who anointed Jesus in the home of the Pharisee. Thus Anselm conceives himself as a present sinner praying to one who in her past was known as a sinner.

> St. Mary Magdalene,
> with a spring of tears,
> you came to the spring of mercy, Christ,
> from whom your burning thirst was abundantly refreshed,
> through whom your sins were forgiven,
> by whom your bitter sorrow received joyful consolation.
> My dearest lady,
> through your own experience you know
> how a sinner can be reconciled to its creator.
> [You also know] what counsel will help a soul in misery,
> what medicine will restore the sick to health.
> This is enough for us to know,
> dear friend of God,
> whose sins, many though they were,
> were forgiven her, because she had loved much.
> Most blessed lady,
> I, the most wretched of [all God's people],
> call to mind your sins, not as a reproach,
> but as a way to experience the abundant mercy,
> by which they were blotted out....
> Therefore, beloved lady, chosen of God,
> in my misery I pray to you in your happiness,
> in my darkness I turn to you for light,
> in my sinfulness, I seek salvation,
> in my uncleanness, I ask for purity.
> Remember, lady most generous,
> what you once were
> and what mercy you so dearly needed.

Ask for me the same forgiveness you [once] needed for
   yourself.
Obtain for me a heart pierced of love [*compunctionem
   pietatis*].
[Obtain also] the gift of humble tears,
a desire for the heavenly homeland,
a disdain for this land of exile,
the anguish of repentance,
the fear of eternal punishment.
Gain for me, beloved,
that easy approach you had and still have
to the springs of mercy.
Draw me there, that he may wash away my sins.
Bring me to him, that I may slake my thirst.
Pour over me the water that will soak into the dryness of my
   soul.
For it is not difficult for you
to obtain whatever you wish
from your beloved Lord and friend who lives and reigns
   forever.

At this point in the prayer Anselm recalls the events of
Scripture which in the tradition of his day are attached to her
story. It is actually a conflation of several stories: the unnamed
sinful woman whom Jesus defended against the "proud Pharisee" (Luke 7:36–50), Mary, the sister of Martha, whom Jesus
"excused" when her sister "complained" (Luke 10:38–42) and
"praised" when Judas "complained" (John 12:1–8), and Mary
Magdalene, who wept at the tomb and then met the Risen Jesus
in the garden (though at first she did not recognize him).

What shall I say,
or how shall I describe
the burning love that moved you at the tomb
to weep for him as you sought him
and to seek him even as you wept?
How indeed describe the indescribable and loving way
he consoled you and inflamed your heart the more?

> How tell the way he hid from you as you tried to see him
> and showed himself when you did not expect to see him?
> How he was present when you sought him,
> and was seeking you when you wept.

As he so often does in the prayers, Anselm now directs his prayer to Christ. Why, he asks, do you hide from her who seeks so intently for you? You know that nothing can satisfy her save the sight of you. Have you put aside compassion, now that you have put on immortality?

> Let it not be so, O Lord.
> For you do not despise us mortals
> Now that you have put on immortality.
> For you became mortal [for the very reason]
> That you might make us immortal.

The prayer dwells on the wonderful recognition scene in the garden, when Magdalene's grief is changed into joy as the Risen One calls her by name: "Mary." It speaks of her mission to be apostle to the apostles when she announces to them: "I have seen the Lord and he said these things to me."

The prayer concludes on a note of introspection and a plea that he be set on fire by the love of sweet Jesus and finally enter into his glory.

> But how dare I, wretched as I am and without love,
> try to express the love of God
> and the love of God's blessed friend?
> For how can my heart emit a fragrance of goodness,
> when that fragrance is not within me?
> [Yet] in truth, you know me, you who are truth itself,
> you are my witness, my Lord, my sweet Jesus,
> that I write this out of love for your love
> wanting your love to set my heart on fire,
> so that I may love only you and what you command
> and offer you a contrite spirit,
> "a broken and humbled heart."

Give me, O Lord, in this my exile
the bread of sorrow and tears,
which I long for more than abundance of [earthly] delights.
Hear me in your love
and for the dear merits of her, your beloved Mary,
and of your blessed mother, the greatest Mary of all.
Do not, most beloved redeemer, Jesus,
do not despise the prayer of your unworthy sinner
but come to the aid of this weakling who loves you.
Rid my heart of its laziness and lukewarmness
and through the warmth and ardor of your love
enable me to arrive at the everlasting contemplation of your glory,
you who live and reign with the Father and the Spirit
one God forever and ever. Amen. (S. III, 64–67)

Prayer to St. Benedict

The prayer to St. Benedict is one of the shorter prayers among those that Anselm wrote. It is addressed to the author of the Rule he had pledged himself to live by. Much of the prayer is spent on detailing his failures in fidelity to the Rule of holy Benedict. As is often true in these prayers, Anselm exaggerates his sinfulness. The picture he draws of himself as an unfaithful monk hardly squares with the monk we know from his fellow monks and his students. Yet we must avoid the temptation to see this as affectation or even hypocrisy. In some ways it is the *lingua franca* of holy people. They quite honestly do not see themselves as holy. In fact, their very holiness and closeness to God help them to see what they regard as the feebleness of their efforts to do the will of God. Their very closeness to God forces them to see more clearly the greatness of the Creator and their own insignificance as a creature. Small infractions are often seen as huge betrayals. Anselm begins his prayer to St. Benedict with a plea for help.

Holy and blessed Benedict,
whom heavenly grace endowed
with the rich blessing of great virtue,

not only that you might be raised up
to the glory you desired
and to the blessed rest of your place in heaven,
to the rest of the blessed, to a seat in heaven,
but also that your blessed life
might draw many others to that same blessedness,
that your sweet counsel might rouse them,
your kindly doctrine instruct them,
your wondrous deeds inspire them.
Oh, I say, blessed Benedict,
you, whom God has favored with such great benedictions,
I prostrate myself before you
with all the humility I can muster,
fleeing to you in anguish of soul.
I pour out my prayers to you,
with all the affection I am able to express;
I implore your help
with all the desire I am able to rouse.
For my need is huge and unbearable.
For I profess to lead a life of ongoing conversion,
as I did promise when I took the name and habit of a monk.
But so far removed am I [from this life of a monk]
that my conscience convicts me
of lying to God, to angels, and to all peoples.
Holy Father Benedict, be with me!
Do not, I beg you, be distraught
by my many failings and lies; but hear me
as I confess to you,
and grant me greater mercy
than I have a right to expect. (S. III, 61–64)

After he lists his failures, his prayer becomes more confident. He calls on Benedict as the advocate of monks who has given them a rule of life and will make it his concern to enable them to do what they ought, "so that both you [he prays], because we are your disciples, and we, because you are our spiritual master, may glory in the presence of God, who lives and reigns forever and ever. Amen."

Asceticism Moving toward Contemplation: The First Meditation

There is no doubt that Anselm's prayers are occupied (even overoccupied) with the sinfulness of the petitioner, often expressed in exaggerated and explosive terms. In passing, I wonder how much the rhetoric of this self-abnegation grows out of the Rule of St. Benedict? In any number of places the Rule reminds monks of their sinful ways and urges them to admit with their tongue and also be convinced in their own hearts that they are inferior to all and of less value. The monk is told to humble himself, and say with the prophet: "I am truly a worm, not a man, scorned by people and despised by them" (*Rule,* chapter 7).

This side of Anselm, whatever its source, may not be to our taste as we move into the twenty-first century. I would want to say, though, that a good healthy sense of our sinfulness can be a wholesome step toward authentic spiritual growth. God's love is greater than our sinfulness, but "falling short of the mark," the biblical notion of sin, occurs in our lives perhaps more often then we might wish. Facing our shortcomings in the context of our service of a loving God is by no means a negative attitude. Recently I read a book on spirituality in which certain prayers were offered as helps to reflective praying. One of the prayers suggested was the time-honored Jesus-Prayer: "Lord Jesus Christ, Son of God, have mercy on me a sinner." The author of the book suggested dropping the word "a sinner," because it was too negative. To my mind the suggestion was unfortunate. We are all sinners to a greater or lesser degree. To face this fact is realistic. It need not be negative. True, to overplay sin is to forget the victory of the resurrection. But to trivialize it is to make light of the cross of Christ.

Paradoxically, our sinfulness can bring us closer to God. Jesus tells, in that wonderful fifteenth chapter of Luke, that "there will be more joy in heaven over one sinner who repents than over ninety-nine righteous persons who need no repentance" (15:7). Joan Chittister, in her book on the Rule of St. Benedict, has a fine story relevant to this matter. The story is about a master who explains to his bewildered student why sin brings the sinner closer to God. There is a string that links us to God. Sin cuts that string. Each time we repent God makes a knot in the string. This makes the string shorter and thereby brings the sinner nearer to God. There is also the story, probably apocryphal, but deep in meaning, of St. Jerome. One day God appeared to him and told him: "I want you to give something to me." Jerome protested that he had left all things to follow Christ. What else was there for him to give? God answered him: "Give me your sins so that I may forgive them."

Yet, while I do believe we can learn something very positive from Anselm's concern with sin and human failures, still I need to point out the importance of seeing Anselm's writings as a whole. If the prayers tend to portray the ascetical side of his thought — the wretchedness of the human condition, the need for conversion — they do not ignore the goal toward which that asceticism is directed, namely, the contemplative experience of God. So often, as in the case of the prayer we have just discussed, the prayer begins with the problem of sin, but comes to a conclusion with that problem coming to resolution in the gracious love of God. The prayers are roads to contemplation.

The two parts of the first of the meditations in the *Prayers and Meditations* may be taken as a good example of these two poles of Anselm's reflection. In the first part of the meditation, in a troubled, disturbed expression of grief, bordering on the neurotic, he broods on his "vile," "despicable" sinfulness. In the second part of the meditation a sense of relief calms his troubled spirit, as he reflects on the all-sufficient remedy for sin: Jesus, whose very name shows him as the one who saves from sin. His appeal to this holy name anticipates the devotion to the name of Jesus, expressed, for instance, in St. Bernard's prayer: "Jesu, dulcis memoria." Here is the concluding part of the first meditation in *Prayers and Meditations*.

> Who will snatch me from the hands of God?
> Who shall be my help, my salvation?
> Who is the one called "the angel of great counsel,"
> the one called savior, that I may call upon his name?
> It is JESUS, yes, JESUS himself.

He is the judge between whose hands I tremble.
But breathe now a sigh of relief, O sinner,
yes, breathe a sigh of relief, and do not despair.
Hope in him whom you fear.
Flee to him from whom you fled.
Insistently invoke the one whom your pride provoked.
JESUS, JESUS, because of that name treat me according to
   that name.
JESUS, JESUS, ignore the proud man who provokes you,
see only the wretched one who invokes you.
Sweet name! Name full of delights!
Name that comforts sinners and brings them blessed hope.
For what is Jesus if not savior?
Therefore, JESUS, because of who you are, be JESUS for me.
You who fashioned me, let me not perish.
You who redeemed me, let me not be condemned.
You who created me in your goodness,
let not the work of your hand perish in its sinfulness.
I ask, O most kindly one,
that my iniquity may not destroy what your goodness
   created.
Recognize, most gracious one, what is yours in me
and blot out what is not yours.
JESUS, JESUS, have mercy on me, while there is time for
   mercy,
lest I be damned when it is time for judgment.
For what good is my blood, if I descend into eternal
   corruption?
For the dead do not praise you, O Lord,
nor those who descend into Sheol.
If you let me into the wide embrace of your mercy,
it will not be narrowed because of me, Oh Lord.
Admit me therefore, O dearest JESUS,
admit me among the number of your elect,
so that with them I may praise you, enjoy you, and glory in
   you
among all those who love your name,
you who with the Father and the Holy Spirit
shall be glorified through endless ages. Amen. (S. III, 76–79)

If any have further doubts about this very positive element of Anselm's spirituality, they need only search out the ideas in the *Monologion* and the *Proslogion.* In these works, and especially in the latter, we see his movement from asceticism to contemplation, as he confronts in a meditative and joyful way the God who was continually drawing him to the divine self.

Texts for Further Reflection

Help me to believe, to hope, to love, to live,
as you know I ought
and as I so earnestly desire. (S. III, 5)

Help me to love you, pray to you,
praise you, meditate on you. (Ibid.)

Most merciful Lady,
overwhelmed as I am by fear and dread
whose intercession should I implore,
but hers whose womb encompassed
the world's reconciliation? . . .
When I have sinned against the son,
I have hurt the mother,
nor can I offend the mother without hurting her son.
Sinner, what then will you do,
sinner, where will you flee?
for who can reconcile me to the son
when his mother is my enemy?
Or who will make me pleasing to the mother,
when the son is angry with me?
But even if both of you are offended in equal measure,
can you not both be merciful [also in equal measure]?
So the one who pleads guilty before the just God
flees to the loving mother of the merciful God.
The one who pleads guilty before the mother he [she] has
    hurt
flees to the loving son of a gentle mother.
The one who pleads guilty moves from one to the other,
throwing himself [herself] between

the loving son and the loving mother. (S. III, 15–16)

Gracious Lord, spare the servant of your mother;
gracious Lady, spare the servant of your son.
Good son, restore harmony between your servant and your
   mother;
good mother, reconcile your servant to your son.
When I throw myself
between the immense graciousness of you both,
may I not fall into great punishment instead.
good son, good mother,
let me not confess this truth about you in vain,
nor blush for hoping in your mercy.
For I love the truth I confess about you,
and I pray for the mercy which I hope for from you.

                                                  (S. III, 16–17)

John, John,
If you are that disciple whom Jesus loved,
I beg you, through that very fact,
let me be, through your intercession,
that sinner whom Jesus forgives. (S. III, 44)

And you, my good leader, my sweet master,
O gentle blessed father Benedict, to you I pray.
I beg you, through the mercy you have shown to others
and the mercy God has shown to you,
show me your mercy in my misery,
for I take joy in your happiness....
Lift me up when I fall,
hold me up when I waiver,
arm me with weapons of the spirit, when I seem
   defenseless.
Teach me and protect me when I must do battle.
Bring me to victory and lead me to victory's crown.

                                                  (S. III, 63–64)

Chapter 2

God: Contemplating the Divine with St. Anselm

The monks appealed "to Anselm to get down in writing what has no doubt made them eager in their fleeting conversation — as if, in returning to the solitude of their prayer cells, they would like to be able to take Anselm with them." —GREGORY SCHUFREIDER

I remember the precise moment, one day in 1894, as I was walking along Trinity Lane, when I saw in a flash (or thought I saw) that the ontological argument is valid. I had gone out to buy a tin of tobacco; on my way back, I suddenly threw it up in the air, and exclaimed as I caught it: Great Scott, the ontological argument is sound! —BERTRAND RUSSELL

I am writing this just after seeing the first episode of a television series called *Nothing Sacred*. The central character is a young priest, likeable, hot-headed, committed to ministry, struggling with personal problems, especially with problems of faith. This first episode manages in the course of one hour to put him in the midst of practically all the "issues" that priests have to deal with today. Father Ray of this film is no "Going My Way" priest. He is deeply human, wholesomely candid, as he struggles to discover what it means to be a priest. One of his struggles has to do with what we today would call the "problem of God." Directed by his bishop to preach about St. Thomas Aquinas's "proofs" for the existence of God, he finds Aquinas unconvincing. Father Ray says, in his sermon: "I can't prove there's a God. But I do get glimpses of God now and then. That's the best I can do — and that's faith. If you're looking for proofs, you're in the wrong business."

As I watched this show, I wondered (since I was in the process of writing about Bec's famous abbot) how Anselm would have reacted to this sermon. I think he would have appreciated the candor of this young priest. Moreover, he would have agreed that you cannot prove the existence of God *from scratch*, as it were. Faith comes first. "Glimpses of God now and then" are the experience of faith. What distinguishes the eleventh-century abbot from this young priest of the late twentieth century is, among other things, the conviction on Anselm's part that one who comes to faith can use reason to understand faith. In fact, one can use reason to show the necessity of what faith believes. If you are able to show the necessity of what you believe, then you are "proving" what you believe. Would Father Ray have understood Anselm? I'm not sure. But I do think that he would have been closer to him than to the nineteenth-century apologists who were convinced that one could offer proofs for the existence of God quite apart from faith. Reason, these apologists felt, could go it alone, as it were, in offering proofs. Cardinal Basil Hume, archbishop of Westminster, in an article in a recent *London Tablet* quotes a saying of George Braque: "Les preuves fatiguent la verité." He suggests it might be translated: "Proofs or arguments obscure the truth" or perhaps "Proofs can make truth tedious."[1] Anselm used reason effectively, but he was ever the man of faith.

The two early writings of Anselm that rank as his most ambitious and creative works, composed during his time at the monastery of Bec, are the *Monologion* and the *Proslogion*. Each of these constitutes, in its own way, an extended inquiry into the existence and the nature of God. These two works definitively establish Anselm's credentials as a remarkable thinker and writer. Like the prayers, they are introspective, but that introspection has a different direction: it is turned toward God, the ultimate goal of the spiritual life.

---

1. *London Tablet,* March 7, 1998, 304.

Like many of his writings, they came into being at the request of his fellow monks. The monks had often and eagerly requested him to put into writing some of the things about God and related topics that he had discussed with them in his many conferences.

We don't know a great deal about Anselm's way of teaching. One cannot escape, though, the conclusion that he loved to talk. He needed an audience of congenial listeners in order to develop his thinking. Southern, writing about the reactions of various monks who heard his conversations, says: "they all said the same thing — his talk was irresistible."[2] If we can believe Eadmer, he was also indefatigable. "He wore out almost all his listeners.... We can unhesitatingly affirm of him what was said of St. Martin that 'the name of Christ or of justice or whatever else belongs to the way of true life was always on his lips'" (*Vita Anselmi*, 14).

Just in passing, I find it interesting that Eadmer singles out "justice" as one of the elements of a true way of life that Anselm would describe. This reference to justice reminds me of an interesting conversation between Anselm and Lanfranc at Canterbury after Lanfranc had been installed as archbishop. Lanfranc had experienced some difficulty in adapting to the mentality of the English. He spoke with Anselm about a former archbishop of Canterbury, Elphege by name, whom the people venerated as a saint and as a martyr. Lanfranc had ordered his name removed from the list of saints because he did not believe that Elphege could be called a martyr, since he had not died for Christian faith. Rather he went to his death because he refused to let his people pay a ransom for his release from the invading Danes. His refusal was based on his realization that if his people paid the ransom, they would be reduced to the state of beggary. Anselm insisted to Lanfranc that Elphege should be honored as a martyr. He was a martyr for justice, as St. John the Baptist was a martyr for truth.

The repeated appeal from his monks to put his spoken word into writing suggests a ready and animated audience: an audience that wanted to become readers, even to the point of making

2. *St. Anselm: A Portrait in a Landscape*, 119.

their own copies of what he wrote. At times he took advantage of the abbot's right to substitute his own words for the reading that would normally take place at dinner time. His disciples afterward recalled what he had said, wrote down the words they remembered, and circulated them.[3] Letter 207 is an interesting example of how eager his listeners were to have copies of his talks. Malchus had been consecrated by Anselm as bishop of Waterford in Ireland on December 28, 1096. Deeply moved by a sermon Anselm had delivered at meal time to the monks of Canterbury when he was there preparing for his consecration as bishop, Malchus wrote later from Waterford to Anselm, who then was in exile, reminding him of a request he had made earlier:

> I already asked you to have written down by dictation the sermon on the Incarnation of our Lord Jesus Christ which you gave us during the meal on the feast of St. Martin [November 11], when you refused a repast of meat in order to feed us with a spiritual repast. (*Letters,* 2:150)

A letter of Anselm to Conus, a monk at Arras, probably written from Bec also while Anselm was in exile, demonstrates Anselm's readiness to speak in congenial company. Conus had been in Anselm's company when he spoke of the three different kinds of pride. He had forgotten two of them and wrote to Anselm asking him to refresh his memory. Anselm replies with a detailed explanation, suggesting that Conus read the material carefully and often so as to understand it more fully. (This letter I will discuss later in chapter 3.)

It can be said, therefore, that in no small measure much of his writing (the early writings at least) exist because of the insistent pleadings of those who heard him speak. Thus, it is to the monks of Bec that we are indebted for having in writing Anselm's two masterpieces of meditation on the nature of God.

Who were the monks, especially those at Bec, who requested Anselm to put in writing what he had said to them in conversation? We can't be sure, but it makes sense to think that

---

3. Many of these remembrances have been published in *Memorials of St. Anselm,* edited by Schmitt and Southern.

they may well have been young monks who came to the monastery with lots of good will, but also with lots of questions,
perhaps even doubts, about some of the things they had been
told they were obliged to believe. It is not difficult to see in
them an image of young people (including young priests like
Father Ray, as well as some older people too) today with similar
problems. I suggest that what he had to say to his monks in the
eleventh century can speak to men and women today grappling
with the perennial questions that inevitably arise in the minds
of those who strive to live fully the Christian life. No question
is more substantive than the question of God. The popularity of
books like Karen Armstrong's *A History of God* and Jack Miles's
God: A Biography witness to people's desire and need to grap-
ple with the "problem of God." Looking at selections from the
Monologion and the *Proslogion* will best serve our spiritual needs
if we see them addressed, not just to monks, but to women
and men like ourselves who often must struggle with questions
and doubts, as we journey, not always by the most direct route,
toward the God of our hopes.

The monks not only asked him to put his conversations in
writing; they also suggested to him the format they hoped he
would follow. They asked that nothing in Scripture be put forth
on the authority of Scripture alone, but that the truth be expressed clearly and simply in plain language with intelligible
arguments. Despite his disclaimer that he was hardly equal to
the task, it's not difficult to imagine that it was a methodology that he embraced with enthusiasm. One cannot help but
wonder: did they imbibe this methodology from Anselm's conversations and were they, in their suggestion of a way for him
to proceed, simply giving back to him what they had learned
from him?

This placing of brackets around the Word of God must have
seemed risky in Anselm's day. Even more risky was his promise
to proceed *sola ratione* (by reason alone). The familiar argument
often used to squelch the new: "we have never done that before" could easily have been invoked against him. Indeed, it
seems clear that the one he called master and father, Lanfranc,
was disposed to differ with him precisely on these terms. Anselm sent the *Monologion* to Lanfranc, asking for suggestions

and inviting him to give a definitive title to the work. Lanfranc offered no praise for the work, citing disapprovingly the lack of any use of authority. Nor did he offer any suggestions for naming the work. From that time on, though he continued to speak with reverence of his one-time teacher, Anselm knew that their paths had diverged. He had set himself on a new course from which there was no turning back.

Anselm was undecided about the name for the earlier of these two works, and Lanfranc had offered no help. His working title had been "An Example of a Way to Meditate on the Reasonableness of Faith." This, however, was more a description than a proper title. He tried the somewhat awkward mix of Greek and Latin, the *Monoloquium*, finally settling on the more refined *Monologion*. The title involves a speaking (*logos*), carried on alone (*monos*). It is a "monologue" in which the speaker reasons with himself.

The second of these works also went through several stages on its way to a final title: (1) "Faith Seeking Understanding" (*Fides quaerens intellectum*), (2) *Sololoquium,* and at last (3) *Proslogion.* The final title combines the Greek *logos*, "word," and the preposition *pros*, which means "to" or "in front of," "in the presence of." The author speaks to himself, to us, to God and in the presence of God.

The *Monologion*

Eadmer tells us of the origin of the *Monologion*:

> He also composed another small book which he called the *Monologion* because in this he alone spoke and argued with himself. Here, putting aside all authority of Holy Scripture, he inquired into and discovered by reason alone what God is, and proved by invincible reason that God's nature is what the true faith holds it to be, and that it could not be other than it is. (*Vita Anselmi*, 29)

There are indications that Anselm himself was not completely satisfied with the *Monologion*. In the preface to the

Proslogion he describes his earlier work as something he wrote at the earnest entreaties of a number of his brother monks. He intended it as an example of someone like himself meditating on the meaning of faith, as he silently reasoned with himself about matters of which he was ignorant. But after having written it and reflecting on its complexity, he began to ask himself if there might not be one single argument that would require nothing other than itself to prove that God exists and that he is the Supreme Good, needing no other and needed by all else that is.

The question became an obsession with him. Eadmer tells us that it took away his desire for food and drink and sleep. It even disrupted his attentiveness to the monastic prayer in chapel. Then one day in that very chapel, while saying matins with the rest of the monks, he experienced a mighty distraction that proved to be a great grace from God. Eadmer tells us about it: "Suddenly one night during matins the grace of God illuminated his heart, the whole matter became clear to his mind and a great joy and exultation filled his inmost being" (*Vita Anselmi*, 90).

After receiving so great a grace, Anselm tells us in the preface to the *Proslogion,* he decided to put it in writing. The experience had brought him such profound joy that he hoped it would give pleasure to those who might read it. He describes it as the work of a person striving "to elevate his mind to the contemplation of God and seeking to understand what he believes."

The *Proslogion*

It is, I believe, to the *Proslogion* we must turn to discover Anselm the monk, the Christian philosopher, the man of prayer, at his very best. Gregory Schufreider is right on target when he suggests that the rational and mystical dimension of Anselm's writing *persona*

> come together in one text [the *Proslogion*] in a way they had not before and never would again in his corpus — per-

haps never would again in the history of Western thought. For the *Proslogion* is a distinctive kind of work, is, we might say, a kind of philosophical prayer book, and thus it offers a form of writing better suited to the rational mysticism that is intent on securing a vision of God than any of the other works Anselm would write.[4]

We need to be clear as to Anselm's purpose in writing these two works. He is not writing what a later age would call "apologetics," that is to say, he is not trying to prove the truths of faith by reason. Rather he is presenting the truths of faith and simply showing that they make sense to a reasonable person. More than that, he wants to make clear that reasoning about these truths will make them shine all the more brightly. In inviting his monks to read his meditations, he is not asking them to depart from the ordinary meaning that reading (*lectio*) enjoyed in the monastic routine. Read these prayers and meditations, he suggests, as you are accustomed to read the Scriptures. Not that he is putting his work on a par with the Scriptures. He is simply expressing his conviction that *sola ratione* (setting Scripture aside for the moment), he can construct a vision of God that can be fruitfully approached in the same way of reading, meditating, and praying that monks (or anyone else for that matter) were accustomed to use in reading the Scriptures. Anselm never swerved from his firm confidence in the total compatibility of Scripture correctly interpreted and reason properly used. It is important, however, to understand that, while he is putting the authority of Scripture aside for the moment and proceeding by reason alone, he is not setting faith aside, as if he were acting as a pure rationalist. Rather faith is the starting point from which he will proceed. But faith doesn't cease to be faith when it is supported by reason.

Clearly for Anselm the Christian, faith takes priority over reason. While there is a content to faith, it is not a series of cold abstractions; instead it is that which his heart "believes and loves." It is assent to God who speaks to us, not merely assent to a series of propositions.

---

4. Schufreider, *Confessions of a Rational Mystic*, 97.

Did reason have a role to play prior to faith? Anselm would never have denied this, but he would make quite clear that reason would exercise that role only for unbelievers. For believers reason adds nothing to the certitude of their faith. What it does bring is greater clarity and greater joy. Nor do believers approach faith through reason; rather faith itself leads to understanding. Indeed for Anselm faith properly speaking is understanding: understanding which brings clarity — and joy. In a letter to Fulk, the bishop of Beauvais, Anselm writes:

> Our faith has to be defended by reason against the impious, not against those who admit rejoicing in the honor of being called Christians. Of these one can justly demand that they hold unshaken the pledge given in baptism; but the former must be shown by reason how irrationally they scorn us. A Christian should progress through faith to understanding, not reach faith through understanding or, if he cannot understand, fall away from faith. Indeed, someone who can attain understanding should rejoice, but someone who cannot understand, should venerate what he is unable to comprehend.[5]

Anselm offers no formal definition of faith. What seems clear is Anselm's belief that faith is possible without any prior rational preparation or justification. More than that, he would maintain that reason's only function for the believer is to understand what is already believed. As Gordon Leff has written:

> [Anselm] allowed reason no independent validity.... Reason was an instrument in demonstrating what was already believed; of itself it could not add to certitude, although it could give additional evidences of its truth. ...Anselm held to the maxim: "If you do not believe you will not understand." Reason, therefore, could never be more than a meditation upon faith, and it always presupposes it.[6]

---

5. Letter 136, *Letters*, 1:315.
6. *Medieval Thought from St. Augustine to Ockham*, 99.

For the believer there are levels of faith: first, there is the gift of simple faith, which is a gift of God and which has no need of reason; second, there is faith that is understood through reason. Both prepare us for what is impossible in this life: the full vision of God to which faith yields place.

If I understand Anselm correctly, simple faith should not be thought of as a faith without content. Simple faith is a way of experiencing God that brings joy, peace, and serenity. Clearly something about God is grasped, though not reasoned about. Mary Ellen Chase, the American novelist, in her book *The Lovely Ambition*[7] describes the attitude toward God of John Tillyard, one of the principal characters in her novel. A Methodist parson, a graduate of Cambridge University, whose ministry brought him from England to the northeast U.S., John Tillyard stated that "he was not interested in trying to prove God's existence which, he said, was impossible and, therefore, a foolish waste of time, or in defining Him, which had been attempted not very successfully through the centuries." Because this was his conviction, when the time came to give a name to his son, he

insisted on calling him Anselm after a saint who, he claimed, had done more for his peace of mind and ways of thought and action than any other philosopher or teacher throughout recorded time. *This Anselm had contended and taught that a simple belief in God would in the end bring some understanding of Him; indeed, that no understanding whatever was possible without an initial and perhaps reckless casting aside of all one's unanswerable questions, doubts and fears.*

(34–35, italics added)

Simple belief can bring a deep understanding of God. In a letter he wrote as archbishop of Canterbury to Pope Urban II, "On the Incarnation of the Word," Anselm makes clear the correlation between faith and experience: that faith is indeed a way of experiencing:

---

7. New York: Norton, 1960.

This I say:
one who has not believed, does not understand.
For the one who has not believed
will not have experienced;
and one who has not experienced
will not understand.
For just as the experience of something
surpasses hearing about it,
so the knowledge of experience
surpasses what one knows only by hearing. (S. I, 284)

Grasping the importance Anselm attributes to experience is critical to understanding the full intent of his writings, especially the *Proslogion*.

In the *Monologion* Anselm offers an example of a meditation on the reasonableness of faith. He begins with what he experienced in the world about him. To give but one of a number of examples, the experience of things in the world that are good in varying degrees leads him to that reality which is Goodness Itself. Simply put, he is lifted up from earthly things toward the contemplation of God.

I want to suggest that in the *Proslogion* he starts from the place at which he had arrived in the *Monologion,* namely, the contemplation or the experience of God. Unless this is clearly understood, the fundamental meaning of the *Proslogion* will be missed. As we approach the most famous of Anselmian texts, chapter 2 of the *Proslogion,* I invite the reader to keep in mind the word "experience." To my mind it is an important key for unlocking the door into Anselm's famous argument. I am anxious to turn that key. In fact, I promised earlier that I would do so by introducing the reader to the fascination of a argument that from the eleventh century down to our own time has received attention from philosophers and theologians. Some have accepted it with joy; others rejected it with scorn. But scarcely any age has been able totally to ignore it. It is probably safe to say that, apart from biblical texts, there is no text in the literature of religion that has been more frequently commented on than chapter 2 of the *Proslogion*.

At the heart of the chapter is, first of all, (1) a simple statement about God (without doubt the illumination that came to Anselm during matins in the dead of night in the monastery chapel) and (2) a fairly obvious principle in the light of which the statement about God is discussed.

1. Anselm understands God to be "that than which no greater can be thought." This seems to make eminent sense. Even a person who does not believe in God, like the fool of Psalm 13 who says in his heart there is no God, would at least understand that belief in God does mean believing in one than which a greater cannot be thought. For if a greater could be thought, then what we were calling God would not be God. Anselm's point is that this statement does not by any means exhaust the meaning of God: it is the very least that one must say to identify God.

2. To this simple notion of what God means Anselm applies an equally simple principle, namely, to exist in reality is greater than to exist only in the mind. To illustrate the difference between existing in the mind and existing in reality, Anselm offers the example of painters. When painters initially think of what they are going to paint, they understand that the painting is in their mind. But once the painting has been produced, it exists not just in the mind but also in reality. If the paintings of Fra Angelico had remained only in his mind, the thousands of people who visit the convent of San Marco in Florence would not have been able to enjoy those marvelous masterpieces. Much better, then, that they exist in reality and not simply in his mind.

The core of Anselm's argument is bringing together (1) this notion of what God means and (2) this principle about the greater of two ways of existing. If God is "that than which no greater can be thought," then God must exist in reality and not just in the mind. For if God exists only in the mind, then a greater can be thought: namely, one that exists in reality as well as in the mind. And if a greater than God can be thought, then clearly God would not be "that than which no greater can be thought." Therefore, to say that God is "that than which no greater can be thought" is to say that God must exist in reality.

Does this make sense to you? Does it turn you on to a fresh and fruitful approach to thinking about God? Perhaps your reaction is: "Well, not really. I can hardly think of praying to 'that than which no greater can exist.' " Of course not! But how about praying about "that than which no greater can exist"? I suggest this, because this is exactly what Anselm was doing when he wrote chapter 2 of the *Proslogion.* In fact, the *Proslogion* in its entirety is one long prayer to God. Anselm is proving the existence of God as he talks to God in prayer. I have attached the entire chapter 2 to this chapter as appendix 1 (p. 106 below), but let me show you how the chapter begins:

> Therefore, Lord, you who give me an understanding of faith,
> give me, insofar as you deem it good for me,
> that I may understand
> that you do exist as we believe you to exist,
> and that you are what we believe you to be.
> And indeed we believe that you are
> that than which no greater can be thought. (S. I, 101)

There is much dispute about what precisely constitutes the starting point of Anselm's argument for the existence of God. Does he begin with an idea of God and then proceed to show that that idea necessarily includes God's existence? What is the source of the statement: "that than which no greater can be thought"? Would Anselm think of it as a definition of God? Is he moving from the logical order to the ontological, i.e., from the order of mind to the order of being? And is such a move legitimate? Is he confusing logical necessity with ontological necessity? Is Anselm simply saying that if you think of God, your thought must include the notion of existence? But does the fact that your thought about God includes existence actually prove that God exists in reality? Just reflecting on these questions helps us to see why this argument has attracted so much attention through the years. It is one of those arguments of which it can be said: "Now you see it, now you don't!" It fascinates because at one moment it seems to demand your acceptance; at another, it calls for skepticism. Commenting on this short passage in the *Proslogion,* David Knowles writes:

Though the language of each clause [of the argument] is pellucid and the meaning of the words perfectly clear, very few readers will succeed in mastering the argument at a glance, and many will have an uneasy feeling that a logical sleight of hand has been brought off at their expense. They need not be ashamed of their bewilderment. A glance at the voluminous literature debating this argument, together with the contrary judgments that have been passed upon it, and the consequent mutual charges between scholars of misunderstanding and misrepresenting Anselm, would seem at least to show that the layman's sense of frustration is not due solely to lack of intelligence.[8]

At this point, I would like to invite you, the reader, to reflect on the argument and mull over the meaning it may have for you. I have read a number of commentaries on it. My own feeling is that we need to remember the context out of which the argument came into being. The argument is articulated in the form of a prayer. Anselm is talking about the existence of God; but we must not forget, as I pointed out earlier, that he does so while speaking to God. The entire *Proslogion* is one long sustained prayer. More than that, the argument emerged from a moment of enlightenment that occurred in a time of prayer. It seems to make sense to me to say that the argument starts, not from an idea or a definition of God, but from an experience of God. (Recall that earlier I suggested keeping the word "experience" in mind, as we try to understand the *Proslogion*.) The argument is an attempt to understand the contemplative intuition that came to him as he prayed matins with his brother monks. As Thomas Merton has written:

In Anselm there is no divorce between intelligence and mysticism. They are one and the same thing. Intelligence springs from mystical intuition and seeks to deepen its religious meaning in an act of homage to the truth. For

---

8. *The Evolution of Medieval Thought*, 103.

Anselm reason serves adoration, and is not mere logic-chopping. The "argument for the existence of God" is itself an act of worship that takes place in the presence of God who reveals himself to the contemplative as the One beyond all comparison, whose Being is absolutely necessary. . . . The *Proslogion* is a monastic meditation born of a profoundly monastic experience.[9]

Later, in the same article, Merton makes the point that Anselm's argument has no utilitarian purpose. He is not trying to convince anyone. He is rather bringing to the joy and serenity of faith "the further joy and clarity of understanding the evident truth" (ibid., 252). Years later, in writing the *Cur Deus Homo* (*Why God Became Human*), Anselm has Boso, his partner in the dialogue, ask him to clarify things which nonbelievers do not accept. But the reason Boso gives for his request is significant: it is not that he may be confirmed in faith (as if he needed such confirmation), but that he may take deep joy in what he already firmly believes (see ibid.)

We do Anselm a disservice when we try to turn him into a nineteenth-century apologist! He would have heartily agreed with Thomas Merton, who writes in *No Man Is an Island:* "A person of sincerity is less interested in defending the truth than in stating it clearly, for he thinks that if truth be clearly seen it can very well take care of itself" (195). More than that, the truth clearly stated does something wonderful for the believer. It was always Anselm's conviction that understanding faith brings joy and comfort to the one who believes. To me this is the intent of the *Proslogion:* helping those who believe to take joy in what they believe.

This basic message of the *Proslogion* can speak to all of us. It is so easy to see faith as a body of abstract truth-formulas to which we give a joyless assent; or, worse still, to see the faith of the Gospel as an announcement of burdens and responsibilities we had better assume, if we want to enter the gates of paradise. This can so easily happen in a culture that lives at a one-dimensional level: a culture that all too easily reduces joy

---

9. "St. Anselm and His Argument," 243.

to superficial gratification and fails to understand the true joy that is the fruit of human growth. And human growth comes from in-depth experience, from a profound experience of what we believe. The truest source of joy is faith. St. Paul writes to the Romans: "May the God of hope fill you with all joy and peace in believing" (15:13). Faith begets joy, because it is the surest way to reach God this side of the great divide. And, Anselm would be eager to tell us, reason seeking to deepen faith's understanding can bring an added measure of joy.

Would this understanding of faith — as an experience to be enjoyed — be helpful to women and men in today's world, beset as they are by questions and problems about faith? I honestly don't know. The reader can answer for herself or himself. I would simply say that a healthy understanding of faith and of the joy that can accompany it may very well help a person to transcend questions and doubts or even to live with them and discover that they are not destructive of faith. Indeed, they may even be the condition of its growth. Faith brings joy because it puts us in touch with God who is the source of joy. Thomas Merton has written: "Faith is not just the grim determination to cling to a certain form of words, no matter what may happen.... Above all it is the opening of an inward eye, the eye of the heart, to be filled with the presence of Divine light."[10]

In understanding Anselm's argument it will be helpful to look at chapter 3 of the *Proslogion*. Scholars disagree as to whether or not it is a continuation of chapter 2 or an independent argument for the existence of God. Since the original text of Anselm was not divided into chapters and since his expressed intention in this work was to put forward "one single argument" for the existence of God that would need nothing other than itself, it seems to make sense to see chapter 3 as a continuation of chapter 2. Chapter 3 distinguished between (1) something that *can* be thought *not to exist* and (2) something that *cannot* be thought *not to exist*. The second clearly is greater than the first. The first refers to creatures, the second to the Creator. The conclusion to which the chapter points is that *that*

---

10. Thomas Merton, *New Seeds of Contemplation* (New York: New Directions, 1962), 129–30.

something than which a greater cannot be thought exists so truly, so fully, so completely that it cannot be thought not to exist. At this point, continuing the prayer-mode, Anselm declares:

> And this "something" is none other than you, my Lord God.
> Thus it must be said that you truly exist, my Lord God,
> so that you cannot be thought not to exist. And rightly so.
> For if someone could think of something better than you,
> this would mean that the creature would be raised above the
>   creator
> and would judge the creator —
> which is patently absurd.
> In fact, whatever else exists besides you alone
> can be thought not to exist.
> Therefore of all things you alone exist most truly and to the
>   highest degree,
> For whatever else exists does not exist as truly as you,
> and therefore has existence in a much lower degree.
> Why then has the fool said in his heart,
> "There is no God"
> when it is so clear to the rational mind
> that you exist to the highest possible degree?
> Why indeed unless because he is stupid as well as foolish?
>
> (S. I, 102–3)

Notice how, while using reason to understand what he believes about God, *Anselm never forgets that this reasoning is in the form of a prayer.* It is in fact an act of worship. He makes clear to us that he is addressing himself to God and praising God. This is to say that what Anselm is offering us is not simply a logical argument, but rather a spiritual experience. He is expressing his excitement and delight at the illumination that came to him as a distraction in the night. Unless this is understood, Anselm's intent is completely missed. What he feels to be true in his experience his reason affirms to be a logical deduction from his initial understanding of "that than which no greater can be conceived."

I hope that you, the reader, have been able to share some of that excitement and delight that Anselm experienced. Yet I realize that this is probably not the kind of prayer you are used to! Nor are the words such that would come readily to mind when you choose to pray. I should remind you once again that Anselm never intended his prayers to be "prayed" by the reader, as if this must be the reader's way of speaking with God. No, on the contrary, he intended that his prayers should stir us to our own prayers. He wants his prayers to move us to the recognition of the ONE who alone perfectly and totally exists. This will not dictate what our prayer should be, but it will purify and deepen what our prayer can become. The *Proslogion* helps us to understand what it means to be a creature, standing in total dependence before the ONE who alone makes us to be and who alone keeps us in being.

Clearly, then, when Anselm speaks about the existence of God — something he believes in faith and intends to understand more fully through reason — he is not talking about just an ordinary kind of existence. *God's existence is the only existence that is uniquely and ultimately real.* God's existence is, therefore, the sole basis for all else that exists.

That is why it would be ridiculous to think of "God" as a concept. Anselm's "that than which no greater can be thought" is not a presupposition for his reasoning, but a *revelation* that forms the subject of his reasoning. It is the revelation of a Name — a Name that Anselm experienced in prayer. We are reminded of the Name ("I am who am") revealed to Moses in the theophany that took place in the desert. In both cases the Name is at the same time a revelation. More than that, it is a Name that reveals a prohibition akin to the first commandment of the decalogue. We are prohibited from thinking of a greater than God. Why? Because God is precisely that than which no greater can be thought. Karl Barth writes:

> How do we know that God's real name is *quo maius cogitari nequit?* We know it because this is how God has revealed himself.... Standing before God we know that we do not stand as any one being before any other being, but as a creature before his Creator. As such and from him who stands over against us, we do not fail to hear this Name

of God and we unhesitatingly accept the prohibition it expresses.[11]

A world where self-sufficiency is the goal of so many lives, where control is admired and dependence frowned upon, where rich nations impose their will on poorer ones, where people of wealth have influence and the poor have none — such a world needs to realize the poverty of its own reality. Our existence is precarious: it is only what is of God in us that enables us to be. Only God can be described as that than which no greater can be thought. Quite literally, apart from God we do not exist. If God were "to let go," even for an instant, we would simply cease to be. Still, if we accept our existential poverty and our total dependence on God, we need have no fear. For God's promise to Moses at the burning bush, "I will be with you," is a promise that is contained in God's very name. It is meant for all of us. The familiar passage from Isaiah: "I will never forget you, my people . . . " has rightfully been a source of comfort for many people.

Almost immediately Anselm's "argument" was challenged by a fellow Benedictine, Gaunilo, a monk from the monastery at Marmoutier on the Loire. Gaunilo wrote a "Reply on Behalf of the Fool." People, he says, might speak of an island somewhere in the ocean that cannot be found and therefore may be called "The Lost Island." It abounds with riches and delights of all sorts. Gaunilo asks: must one argue, then, that this perfect island must exist, because, if it did not, then any existing island would be more excellent than it. What he is asking, in effect, is this: does an island that can be thought to be perfect have to exist to be perfect? Anselm incorporated Gaunilo's critique and his reply to it in the manuscript of the *Proslogion*. His counterargument makes clear that his words about God do not apply to *any* perfect thing, but only to that *one unique* being who by definition is "that than which no greater can be conceived." He is not talking about just an ordinary kind of existence. He is talking about that Being whose existence alone is uniquely and

---

11. Barth, *Anselm: Fides Quaerens Intellectum,* 152.

ultimately real. It is God's existence that is the sole basis for all else that exists.

If anyone is able to find anything else (i. e., any reality apart from God) to which his argument might be applicable, Anselm promises that he would see to it that that person received a gift of the "Lost Island."

Some Texts for Reflection

From the Monologion

The *Monologion* offers a string of arguments aimed at demonstrating the existence of God from a consideration of the reality of the visible world. Thus, we perceive in the universe things that are good, but good in a greater or lesser degree. We can think of a good tree, a good house, a good book, a good person. All these realities, as well as others we might mention, are good — but only in a limited way. The goodness of the tree is not the goodness of the house. None of these goods is good with the fullness of what goodness means. They only share goodness; they are not goodness itself. For this reason, they are not adequate in themselves to account for the goodness that they possess. But it is unthinkable that that goodness should go unaccounted for. Reason, therefore, moves us to conclude that there must exist an absolute good, from which all these lesser goods derive their goodness. This absolute good must exist as a Reality that is good, not in virtue of another, but precisely in virtue of itself. Listen to Anselm in chapter 1 of the *Monologion:*

> Since all desire to enjoy only those things
> which they suppose to be good,
> it is natural that they should at some time
> turn the eye of the mind
> to an investigation of that being
> by which these things are good:
> things which they would not desire,
> if they did not judge them to be good.
> Thus, following the lead of reason,

they will be able to proceed rationally toward those truths
which without reason they would not know....
For who can doubt that that being,
through which all good things are good,
must itself be a great good?
This is to say that this "great good" is good through itself,
whereas all else that is good is good through this "great
    good." (S. I, 13–15)

"Great good" (*magnum bonum*) is a rather clumsy expression. Anselm really is talking about the "highest" good or the "supreme" good. From a consideration of things that *have* goodness, he concludes to the supreme good which *is* goodness.

Worth our reflection in the above text is Anselm's reference to the "eye of the mind." This is an important metaphor for him. The "eye of the mind" is the inner eye whereby one *sees* what cannot be grasped by the external senses. It is what Eastern religions would call the "third eye." For Anselm it is a discerning and discriminating "eye": a way of perceiving not only physical good but also moral and spiritual good. It is the inner eye of consciousness and of conscience. It expands our vision.

If you have ever had an eye examination, you will remember that you had drops put in your eyes. These drops dilated your pupils. When you left the doctor's office, you probably could not see the speedometer of your car. But you could see the headlights of oncoming cars sparkling out in all directions. Traffic signals were like Christmas trees flashing first red, then green lights all around. With your eyes dilated, you could not see what was right before you, but you could see what was beyond you. Your eyes had become like wide-angle lenses. Your vision had been widened, expanded. This expanding of vision may be taken as a kind of symbol of what happens when the inner eye, the eye of the mind, is opened. We see what is beyond normal vision.

Thus it is that, as this "eye" expands into the vision of God, the being of God increases and the being of creatures decreases. Chapter 28 makes this very explicit:

> From the preceding considerations, it seems to follow that this Spirit [God] — who exists in so wonderfully singular and so singularly wonderful a way — in a certain sense alone exists, while other things, seemingly comparable to it, do not exist.

This intuition, shared by the mystical insights of various religions can be made more palatable perhaps by expressing it this way: the Supreme Spirit alone necessarily exists; all else exists contingently. Anselm seems to say this in the conclusion of chapter 28:

> The Creator Spirit alone IS, all creatures are not;
> yet creatures are not entirely nonexistent,
> since through the one who alone exists absolutely,
> they have been made something out of nothing. (S. I, 46)

One is reminded of the words that God is supposed to have spoken to St. Catherine of Siena: "I am the One Who is; you are she who is not."

a. Chapter 15, Talking about God: Anselm is very much aware of the difficulty involved in taking the words we use to describe created reality and using them to describe the Supreme Being. Ultimately God is ineffable. The only stance a creature can assume before God is, in ultimate terms, silence and awe. Our words simply will not do, yet that is all we have.

> I should be surprised,
> if among the nouns and verbs we use
> to describe things made from nothing,
> there would be found any
> which could be properly used
> to describe the Creator of the reality of all things.
> Yet we must try to see
> where reason will lead us in such an investigation.
>
> (S. I, 28)

He makes clear his belief that any term we use in speaking about God is unable to express the divine nature. Even when we try to use terms to show that God is the highest of all beings or greater than all things that have been created, we are still talking about the divine being in terms of God's relationship to created things. We are not describing the nature of God as it is in itself.

It is important that we realize this fact: all our language about God is metaphorical, analogical. What we say about the creator derives from what we experience of God's creation. If we experience "father-love," it is meaningful for us to call God "Father." But if we use only the term "father," we give the impression that this word is able to express the nature of God. We must therefore use many names to refer to God. The Scriptures offer us an abundance of names: father, mother, spouse, shepherd, lover, rock, shield, and more. Each of them is a window looking into the reality of God; none of them separately can exhaust the meaning of God nor can all of them together. If we think that we have found God in our words, thoughts, and definitions, it is not really God we have grasped, but simply our own faltering speech about the divine mystery we must ever be seeking, but will never grasp fully this side of eternal blessedness. Ultimately if we wish to reach God, we must go where reason cannot go: into darkness and silence. Thomas Merton wrote:

> Now, while the Christian mystic must certainly develop, by study, the theological understanding of concepts about God, he is called mainly to penetrate the wordless darkness and apophatic light of an experience beyond concepts. . . . Relinquishing every attempt to grasp God in limited human concepts, the contemplative's act of submission and faith attains to His presence as the ground of every human experience and His reality as the ground of being itself.[12]

b. Chapter 23, God Is Everywhere: In chapter 23 Anselm meditates on the omnipresence of the Supreme Being and points out that it means much more than saying that the Supreme Nature is in a lot of places or even in all places that are.

---

12. Thomas Merton, *Contemplation in a World of Action* (New York: Doubleday Image, 1973), 185.

"Everywhere," he makes clear, transcends all places. Hence "the Supreme Nature is more appropriately said to be everywhere in the sense that it is in all existing things, rather than simply in all places." Even this statement needs to be qualified. It is in all things not as if contained by them, but as containing all by permeating all.

> ...The Supreme Nature, according to the very reality of
>   things,
> is more appropriately understood to be everywhere
> in the sense that it is in all existing things,
> rather than simply in all places.
> ...Further it must be said
> that it is in all things in such a way
> that it is at one and the same time
> totally and perfectly present in each thing that exists.
>
> (S. I, 41–42)

The more we mull over this truth that "God is everywhere," the more remarkable we realize it to be. God is everywhere as the cause of everything that is. God is not confined to certain places, like churches or chapels. There are no privileged places where God is more present than in others. God is totally present wherever God is and where anything at all exists. The psalmist realized there is no escaping from God's presence.

> Where can I hide from you?
> How can I escape your presence?
> I scale the heavens, you are there!
> I plunge to the depths, you are there!...
> You created every part of me,
> Knitting me in my mother's womb.
>
> (Ps. 139: 7–8, 13)

It is a wondrous thing for us to realize that God is here and there and everywhere. God is not a far-away being. God is present anywhere and everywhere by a presence that is unique to God. For God is in all things as their source and sustainer. God is in each one of us. Spirituality is not a matter of being good so that we can find a God who is outside us; rather it is becoming aware of a God within whose love makes us good. As Joan Chittister has put it: "God is within us to be realized, not outside of us to be stumbled upon."[13]

Our God is an immanent God, whose grace continually calls us to conversion, to heartfelt communion with our sisters and brothers, to compassionate concern for the needy, the oppressed, the victims of injustice and prejudice. This happens in our everyday lives. Thus, we do not have a relationship with God in addition to the relationships we have with others. "Our relationship with God is inseparable from every relationship we have. We experience God most completely by experiencing ourselves and other people, and whenever we experience ourselves and other people, we also experience God."[14]

From the Proslogion

a. Chapter 9, Divine Mercy and Goodness:

> O Mercy, from what abundant sweetness and sweet
> abundance,
> you flow over us.
> O Immensity of the divine goodness,
> with what affection must even sinners love you!
> You save the just, as justice does commend;
> you free the unjust, whom justice does condemn.
> The former are saved with the help of their merits;
> the latter are saved despite their lack of merits.
> In the former you recognize the good you have given them;
> in the latter you ignore the evil you hate in them.
> O immense Goodness, so far exceeding what we can
> understand,
> let that mercy descend upon me —
> that mercy which comes forth from you in such wondrous
> abundance.
> Let it flow over me as it flows out from you! (S. I, 107–8)

---

13. Chittister, *The Rule of St. Benedict*, 64.
14. Michael Skelley, *The Liturgy of the World: Karl Rahner's Theology of Worship* (Collegeville, Minn.: Liturgical Press, 1991), 100.

b. Chapter 14:

O my soul, have you found what you were seeking?
It was God for whom you were seeking:
God whom you found to be the highest of all,
that than which no better can be thought;
that which is life itself, light wisdom, goodness,
eternal blessedness and blessed eternity,
that which exists everywhere and always.
But if you have not found your God,
how can this God be what you have found God to be
and what you know [God to be]
with certain truth and true certitude?
But if in truth you have found God,
why do you not experience what you have found?
Why, O Lord God, do I not experience you,
if I have found you? ...
Why is this, O Lord, why indeed?
Is my eye darkened by its own weakness
or dazzled by your glory?
Without doubt it is darkened by its own insignificance
and dazzled by your immensity. ...
For how great is that light from which shines every truth
that enlightens the rational mind!
How great the truth in which is everything that is true!
And outside of which is nothingness and falsehood!
How immense the truth that by a single glance sees all
    creation
and by which and through which and how all was made
    from nothing.
What great purity, simplicity, certitude, and splendor are
    there!
Surely it is more than a creature can understand.

(S. I, 111–12)

c. Chapter 15 is very brief and before offering it for reflection, I want to speak briefly about it. Actually it belongs with
chapter 14 and is a conclusion drawn from it. The conclusion
is important. It appears at first sight to suggest that Anselm's

reflections about God ultimately end up in failure. For chapter 15 states that "that than which no greater can be thought" is greater than can be thought. What he is speaking about in this chapter is the paradox of the mystical experience of God: we know God *by unknowing*. No thought we have can comprehend the vast reality of God; yet we do (or can) experience God. We see, but our seeing is limited. We don't (and cannot) see all. In fact, what we see is so small compared to the immensity of God that it is almost like unseeing. The mystics have used terms like "dazzling darkness." For the mystic is blinded by the dazzling light of God's reality. Thomas Merton has written:

> In mystical experience, God is "apprehended" as unknown. He is realized, "sensed," in His immanence and transcendence. He becomes present not in a finite concept, but in His infinite reality which overflows every analogical notion we can utter of him.[15]

In the same work, Merton says the same thing, but puts it more concretely. He compares our thoughts about God to matches we might light in order to see the sun.

> As soon as we light these small matches which are our concepts: "intelligence," "love," "power," the tremendous reality of God who infinitely exceeds all concepts suddenly bears down upon us like a dark storm and blows out all their flames!
>
> It is dangerous to be able to resist this whirlwind and to keep your matches lighted when the night wind blows in from His dark sea.... It is perilous indeed to be satisfied with a philosophy that makes you ignore the most important consequence of God's transcendence: the necessity of faith. (Ibid., 106–7)

Anselm, I believe, would have found these words of Merton congenial to his own thinking. Faith does indeed enable us to

---

15. Thomas Merton, *The Ascent to Truth* (New York: Harcourt, Brace, 1951), 82–83.

know God; but the knowledge of faith, wondrous though it is, pales into darkness compared to the vision of God that comes to us when we have completed our pilgrim way to the heavenly homeland. Listen to chapter 15 of the *Proslogion:*

> Therefore, Lord, not only are you that than which no greater
>   can be thought,
> but you are "something" greater than can be thought.
> For since it can be thought that there is such a being
> if you were not yourself this being,
> you would not be that than which no greater can be thought.
> But this cannot be. (S. I, 112)

d. Chapter 16 continues this reflection on the "inaccessibility" of God, yet the completeness of God's presence to us and our presence to God.

> In very truth, Lord, this is the inaccessible light
> in which you dwell.
> Nothing else can penetrate it so as to see you there.
> Truly, I see it not: it is too bright for me,
> yet whatever I see I see through it,
> just as the eye, weak as it is, sees through the light of the
>   sun,
> [though] it cannot look at that light in the sun.
> My mind cannot reach that light: it shines too brightly....
> O supreme and inaccessible light!
> O whole and blessed truth!
> How far you are from me, who am so close to you.
> How far removed from my vision are you,
> to whose vision I am so near.
> You are wholly present everywhere,
> yet I see you not!
> In you I move and in you I am,
> Yet I cannot come to you!
> You are within me and around me,
> Yet I do not experience you. (S. I, 112–13)

e. Chapter 18 expresses the frustration he is experiencing in his effort to know God: "I tried to rise to the light of God, instead I fell into my own darkness. In fact not only have I fallen into it, I feel enveloped by it." Yet he is still moved in faith to pray:

> Help me, Lord, for the sake of your goodness.
> It is your face I have sought,
> I must see your face.
> Turn not your face away from me.
> Free me from myself and lift me up to you;
> cleanse, heal, sharpen my attention,
> enlighten the eye of my mind,
> so that it may behold you.
> Let me regain its strength
> and strive toward you, O Lord, with all my mind.
> What are you, Lord, what are you?
> What shall my heart understand you to be?
> Surely you are life, you are wisdom, you are truth,
> you are goodness, you are happiness, you are eternity,
> you are everything that is good. (S. I, 114)

The inaccessibility of God means that we cannot know God as God is in the divine self. We can only catch glimpses of God in the "images" of God that come under our experience. As M. J. Charlesworth has written:

> [Anselm] admits that we cannot speak of God directly, but only "through some similitude or image" [Charlesworth quotes from the *Monologion*, chapter 65]. "We do not see and speak of God by what is proper to God." However, even if what we say about God is not the full truth, it is not thereby false. To deal adequately with this whole question St. Anselm would of course need a theory of analogical predication, such as Aquinas was to develop later.[16]

---

16. Charlesworth, *St. Anselm's Proslogion*, 81.

f. Chapter 26 concludes the *Proslogion* with a beautiful prayer:

> I pray, O Lord, that I may know you, love you, and take my
>   joy in you.
> And if I cannot achieve this fully in this life
> at least let me advance day by day, till that joy comes to its
>   fullness.
> May my knowledge of you progress in this life
> and come to fullness in the next.
> May my love increase here and reach fulfillment there,
> so that here my joy may abound in hope,
> and there find its fullness.
> O Lord, you command us, you counsel us, to call upon you
>   through your Son
> and you promise that [if we do so] our joy shall be full.
> So I call upon you, Lord, through our wonderful counselor.
> May I receive what you promise through your truth
> so that my joy may be full.
> Truthful God, I ask you that I may receive
> so that my joy may be full.
> Meanwhile, let my mind meditate on it;
> let my tongue speak of it;
> let my heart love it;
> let my soul hunger for it;
> let my flesh thirst for it;
> let my whole being desire it:
> until I enter into the joy of my Lord,
> who is three in one and blessed for all ages. Amen.
>
> (S. I, 121)

Appendix 1: Chapter 2 of the **Proslogion**

> Therefore, Lord, you who give me an understanding of faith,
> give me, insofar as you deem it good for me,
> that I may understand
> that you do exist as we believe you to exist,
> and that you are what we believe you to be.
> And indeed we believe that you are
> that than which no greater can be thought.

But could it be said that there is no such reality,
since the fool has said in his heart: "There is no God"?
But surely that same foolish one,
when he hears what I have just said:
"that than which no greater can be thought,"
understands what he hears,
and what he understands exists in his mind,
even if he does not understand that it exists [in reality].
For it is one thing for something to exist in the mind,
quite another to understand that it exists [in reality].
For example, when a painter initially thinks about what he is
     going to paint,
he has it in his mind,
but he does not yet understand it to exist,
since he has not yet painted it.
But once he has painted it,
he has it in his mind and he also understands that it exists
     [in reality].
because he has made it.
Hence even the fool is convinced that there is something in
     his mind,
namely, that than which no greater can be thought,
since he understands what he hears
and what is understood exists in the mind.
However, if that than which no greater can be thought
exists only in the mind,
then that than which no greater can be thought
would be something than which a greater can be thought.
But this is absurd.
Therefore, there can be no doubt that
that than which no greater can be thought
exists both in the mind and in reality. (S. I, 101–2)

Appendix 2: Chapter 4 of the Proslogion

The conclusion of chapter 3, wherein Anselm returns once
more to the fool of Psalm 14 who says in his heart: "There is
no God," prepares the way for chapter 4, which takes up the
"fool's" statement. Here he makes clear the distinction between

the word that is used to designate something and the reality which that word designates. The fool, he tells us, can say the words "God does not exist," but what is "in his heart" does not correspond to the true meaning which those words necessarily express. His words distort the true meaning of the very words he uses. It is impossible for him to think their true meaning, because what he says contradicts that meaning. Listen to Anselm:

> How the fool says in his heart what cannot be thought?
> How can he say in his heart what he cannot think,
> or how can he not think what he says in his heart,
> since to say in one's heart and to think are one and the same?
> But if he really (or rather since he really) thought it:
> (because he said it in his heart);
> yet did not really say it in his heart,
> (because he could not think it),
> it must be that there is more than one way
> in which something can be "in the heart" or "in thought."
> For in one way a thing is thought,
> when [only] the word signifying it is thought.
> In another way [a thing is thought]
> when the very reality which the thing is
> is understood.
> In the first case [where only the word is thought]
> it is possible to think that God does not exist,
> but by no means in the second case [when the reality of God is understood].
> No one who understands what God is
> can think that God does not exist,
> although they may say the words,
> but the words have no meaning
> or [at most] a meaning that is foreign [to the reality].
> For God is that than which a greater cannot be thought.
> Whoever clearly understands this,
> understands that God exists in such a way
> that God cannot not exist even in thought.
> Therefore, whoever understands that God exists in this way

cannot [even] think that God does not exist.
Thanks be to you, good Lord,
for what I have believed through your gift,
I now understand through your enlightenment,
so that even if I did not want to believe that you exist,
I could not fail to understand that you do. (S. I, 103–4)

Appendix 3: The Ballad of St. Anselm

The origin of the following ballad, which I downloaded from the Internet, is unknown. It is accompanied by the suggestion that it may be sung to the tune of "Waltzing Matilda!"

Once a jolly friar got himself an argument
And couldn't get it out of his mind.
He thought that he could prove the existence of the Deity
Because of the way that the words are defined.

Chorus
Thus spake St. Anselm, thus spake St. Anselm,
Thus spake St. Anselm, who now is long dead,
And we're awed as we read his proof so ontological;
Who can deny a word that he said?

If that than which nothing greater can be conceived
Can be conceived not to exist,
Then 'tis not that than which nothing greater can be
    conceived:
This is unquestionable, I insist.

For in that case a being greater can be conceived,
Whose major traits we can easily list:
Namely, that than which nothing greater can be conceived
And which cannot be conceived not to exist.

For if that than which nothing greater can be conceived
Has no existence outside of man's mind,
Then 'tis not that than which nothing greater can be
    conceived,
Due to the way the words are defined.

For in that case a greater can be conceived
(This is of course analytically true);
Namely, that that than which nothing greater can be
  conceived
And which exists in reality too!

Chorus
Thus spake Anselm, thus spake Anselm,
Thus spake Anselm with weighty intent,
And we're awed as we read his proof so ontological.
Would that we could understand what it meant.

This bit of versifying will not find a place in any anthology of poetry, medieval or modern. It does express, however, the mixed feelings which the "ontological" argument generates: a sense of "awe" at its cleverness coupled with a kind of wistful desire, never quite realized, to understand its meaning.

Chapter 3

Friendship and the Communion of Saints

Anselm's goal in friendship was not of this world, even in its most exalted activities; it was nothing less than the kingdom of Heaven — the ultimate goal of all rational beings.

— R. W. SOUTHERN

Since in the exile of this life I am enjoined never to cease encouraging all whom I can to progress toward the heavenly homeland, I surely ought not withhold this service from those to whom I know I am joined by the debt of love.   — Letter 180

One of my favorite tenets of Christian faith is belief in the communion of saints. What I like about it is that it is a very inclusive belief. It's about everybody. What it tells us is that we are all saints — more or less. When I say "more or less," I mean that there are some in that communion whose sanctity is at 100 percent. Our deceased parents, relatives like Aunt Minnie and cousin George, friends we have traveled with along life's road — all of these who have gone to God — they're all at 100 percent.

But the communion of saints isn't just about those who "have made it." It's also about all of us who are trying to. Thinking about this belief challenges us to ask: what percentage are we at — we who are saints more or less? Would you say that most of us are at about 50 percent? Maybe some are much higher — like 80 percent perhaps? Most of us are probably trying, some more eagerly than others, to push up the percentage. Folks who use computers will know that, when you put a new software program into your system, a bar appears at the bottom of the screen. In the bar is a color — red or green or blue — that keeps moving to the right to show what percentage of the program has been installed. It moves from 0 percent to 100 percent. The program Christians are called to put into their lives might well be the beatitudes that begin the Sermon on the Mount in Matthew's Gospel. "Beatitude," one might say, is another name for "saint" or, perhaps I should say, for "sainthood." Saints, Jesus says, the real kind, are pure in spirit: they're not attached to a lot of things. They are meek: they don't insist on always having their own way. They are merciful: truly concerned about other people and their needs (this beatitude's demands might pull quite a number of us — maybe quite a lot of politicians especially — down to a rather low percentage on the sanctity scale). The real saints, Jesus continues in the Beatitudes, are pure of heart: they have a singleness of purpose and a deep unity in their lives. And of course any true saint has to be an instrument of peace: peace in oneself and peace among peoples.

Saints are people who have achieved the goal of spirituality or at least have set their sights on that goal and are moving toward it with courage and determination. Their lives have depth and direction. They have a perception of what really matters in life. They are the kind of people who can change the world. Some of them do.

As we saints on earth strive, with setbacks here and there, to move up that scale of sanctity, the heavenly saints from their 100 percent angle watch us and intercede for us. As they see us inching our way along the sanctity scale, they are cheering for us all the way. They are our best friends, for they will only our highest good.

What about Anselm? He of course has made it. He was canonized probably some time in the twelfth century (we don't know exactly when) and was named a doctor of the church in 1720. Dante added his seal of approval by placing Anselm among the spirits of light and power in the sphere of the sun in the *Paradiso* (canto 12). So there is no question: he is at 100 percent. He is one of those cheering us on to join that heavenly communion. And even before he "made it," he viewed the wondrous friendship that the saints in heaven have with us as a prototype of the kind of friendship that we need to have for one another. Friends are pilgrims traveling together toward the heavenly homeland. What unites them most closely is the love and care they have for one another as they pursue their common goal: getting to 100 percent.

But, if friendship has a goal that is otherworldly, it still is very much a human reality. So before looking at Anselm's views on friendship and as a preparation for doing so, let's briefly reflect on its human dimension. The first thing we need to say is that sanctity does not diminish our humanity; it is rather humanity's flowering. Nor is the pursuit of holiness a solitary venture — even for hermits. We exist with and for others. People need people. To grow we need other human beings. Human "belongingness" is a powerful and healthy need in us. In the oft-quoted words of John Donne:

> No man is an Island, entire of itself;
> every man is a piece of the continent, a part of the
>   main. . . .
> any man's death diminishes me,
> because I am involved in mankind;
> and therefore never send to know for whom the bell tolls;
> it tolls for thee.

Or, to lighten things up with a bit of wacky wisdom from the Internet: "it is well to remember that the entire universe, with one trifling exception, is composed of others."

Human solidarity, "connectedness" with other persons, is a reality we are all conscious of and a need we all experience. For it is in relationships with people that I discover who I am. Being connected to others in the context of some kind of community enables me to become the person I am called to be. In fact, relationship is so important to being a person that, if you could conceive the possibility of someone existing but having absolutely no relationships, that one, I think, would scarcely be a person. For what makes me a person is being joined to others in a network of relationships that make for human unity and wholeness.

Not every relationship is friendship. Some relationships never go beyond that of acquaintanceship. An acquaintance is someone with whom I have had some contact, but for the most part only at a superficial level; or, if one borrows from Ambrose Bierce in *The Cynic's Word Book,* an acquaintance is "a person whom we know well enough to borrow from, but not well enough to lend to."

Friendship is relationship at a level of personal depth. Intimacy is an importance element of friendship. Intimacy means that a friend is someone with whom I can be myself. With a friend I do not have to pretend to be what I am not. For if my friend is a true friend, then he or she accepts me as I am. Emerson expressed it this way: "a friend is one with whom I can be sincere." One ought to make the point, though, that sincerity ought not to be confused with frankness. If we feel it necessary to express disagreement with a friend, we must be careful not to do so in a disagreeable manner. Thus, if your friend has said something that hurts you or that you think was wrong or mistaken, sincerity requires that, if the matter is of any consequence, you speak with your friend about it. Yet sincerity does not call for you to devastate your friend. You don't say: "That was a stupid thing you said. You should know better." Correction of a friend should take place in a loving context. Better to put it this way: "What you said was disturbing to me. I'm sure you did not intend it the way it looked to me. Perhaps we could talk about it." The book of Proverbs says it well:

> A mild answer turns away anger,
> But a sharp word makes tempers rise....
> A soothing word is a tree of life,
> But a mischievous tongue breaks the spirit.
> (Prov. 15:1, 4)

Anselm was probably better than most at the gentle word that turns away anger. He never hesitated to correct a friend when he deemed it necessary, but he was skilled at voicing rebukes in words that left no doubt that he was speaking in love. Examples of this are plentiful in his letters. For instance, he writes to Henry, a monk of Christchurch, Canterbury, asking for an explanation of his failure to visit Bec on his trip to Rome. He informs Henry how his friends, "rejoicing in a false

. hope, awaited your arrival until, suffering real desperation, we learned you had crossed over to England." Clearly Anselm is not pleased with Henry and wants an explanation. But note how graciously he couches it.

> Yet if I know your love well, I do not believe this was done without some reasonable cause. Hence, that no suspicion may remain about your having contempt or slight love for our monastery — which God forbid! — please let me know how I should answer them about why your love passed by and did not visit us.... For just as I want you to do nothing which is not advantageous to you, so I do want no one to imagine anything about you which is not befitting you.
>
> (*Letters,* 1:116)

Even before Dickens wrote his novel *Our Mutual Friend*, the term "mutual" was linked with friendship. In today's market economy, however, it might be that, for some people, "mutual" would more readily be linked with "funds." Mutual funds are investing corporations that carry in their portfolio diversified stocks or bonds. They are diversified in such a way that (hopefully) the common goal of the investors will be achieved, namely, that their investments will be both safe and in process of continual growth. Some of the elements of mutual funds might without too much straining apply to the mutuality that belongs to friendship. Thus, it is fair to say that (1) friends are different from one another, (2) they offer an atmosphere of safety and peace (you don't need to be always on guard with your friend), (3) friends strive together for a common goal, and (4) they contribute to one another's growth.

Much of this understanding of friendship is picked up in Cicero's well-known definition of a friend: "Amicus est tamquam alter idem" (A friend is like another self). *Alter idem* is often translated as "a second self." Yet this does not convey the subtlety of the expression. For *alter* means "other" and *idem* means "same." What Cicero is saying is that my friend is not a "carbon copy" of myself whom I like simply because I find myself there. No, the point he is making is that because a friend is at the same time "other" and "same," friendship creates a dialectic, a kind of healthy tension, without which it would too easily be taken for granted. When my friend is both "other" and "same," the friendship embodies a challenge. I grow *with* my friend because there is a "sameness" between us, that is to say, we prize the many things we have in common (or at least the important things). But also I grow *because* of my friend, since there is in my friend an "otherness" that brings me *insight* that I would otherwise not have and at times a *challenge* that may call me to change and transformation. Emerson wrote of the richness of *alter idem*.

> Friendship requires that rare mean betwixt likeness and unlikeness that piques each with the presence of power and of consent in the other party.... Let [my friend] not cease an instant to be himself. The only joy I have in his being mine is that the not-mine is mine.... Better be a nettle in the side of your friend than his echo.[1]

Friendships can die when the *alter* far exceeds the *idem*. Or it may happen that one friend grows and the other does not. When this happens, the mutuality on which the friendship was built disappears and with it the friendship. Thus, it may be that people who were once friends drift apart and finally discover that they can no longer speak sincerely and truthfully with one another.

Friendships must not be taken for granted. They require an investment of time and energy. They have to be worked at if they are to endure. James Boswell in his celebrated life of Dr. Samuel Johnson quotes his eccentric subject as saying: "If a man does not make new acquaintances as he advances through life, he will soon find himself alone. A man, Sir, must keep his friendships in constant repair."[2]

---

1. Ralph Waldo Emerson, *Essays*, First Series II (Boston: Houghton Mifflin, 1903), 208.
2. See James Boswell, *Life of Samuel Johnson* (1934 ed.), vol. 2 (April 1773), 214.

Anselm's Letters

This background about the meaning of friendship can prepare us as we seek to understand the meaning that friendship had for Anselm. There can be no doubt that friendship was a central experience in his monastic life. Though he wrote no treatise on friendship, we can glean from his writings — most especially from his letters — some idea of what friendship meant to him and the importance he gave to it in the Christian life. While Anselm probably was not acquainted with Cicero, the Ciceronian vocabulary designating a friend as another self appears frequently in one form or another in his letters.

The letters are plentiful: of those between 1070 and 1109 some four hundred have survived. It seems clear, moreover, that Anselm intended them to survive and took precautions to guarantee that they would. Clearly he saw his letters as equal in importance to his other writings. They exhibit the same careful crafting, the same delight in words and the interplay of words as any of his writings. Still, it has to be said that there are times when he can be awfully wordy and repetitive. You have to wonder at times: why does he feel the need to say the same thing over again in different ways? But even if you agree that he sometimes, in fact almost too frequently, uses too many words, you have to admit that he knows how to use words well. Besides exhibiting his writing art, the letters show something of his person as well: his analytic, meditative approach to life, his sensitive temperament, as well as his deep empathy for the well-being of those to whom he writes. Eadmer bears witness to a wisdom and an understanding revealed so clearly in his letters:

> Being thus inwardly more clearly illuminated with the light of wisdom and guided by his power of discrimination, he so understood the characters of people of whatever sex or age that you might have seen him opening to each one the secrets of his heart and bringing them into the light of day. (*Vita Anselmi,* 13)

Anselm the person, the spiritual master, lives in the letters he has left to posterity. They are, as we shall see from a few examples, expressions, often passionate expressions, of deep friendship. He never forgets, though, that friends are important to one another, because they are pilgrims helping one another on the way to the heavenly homeland. Friendships are ways God uses to help us raise the level of our sanctity. Friends rejoice when friends grow in holiness.

It seems clear that he intended some of his letters as brief essays on the life of the spirit and wanted these letters to be used by persons other than the ones to whom they were addressed. For instance in 1104 he writes a letter of encouragement to a young man who had just become a novice at Christchurch Abbey, Canterbury. The young monk, Warner by name, had intellectual gifts which Anselm admired. He writes to him:

> By the grace of God you are well educated. Direct the knowledge which God permitted you to acquire while loving the world toward the love of God, from whom you have whatever you have, so that in place of the worldly glory for which you were longing with your learning you may attain the eternal glory which you either scorned or only feebly desired. Zealously observe the customs of our order which you have entered as though they were decreed by God.
>
> (*Letters*, 3:61)

At this point, rather than giving him advice on the life of a monk, Anselm advises him to ask for the letter he had written to Dom Lanzo, when he had begun his novitiate at the monastery of Cluny. The letter to Lanzo had been written in about 1072 or 1073, more than thirty years earlier. But Anselm expected that it was available for reading by others — a clear indication that he intended his letters to endure.

Friendship was, in Anselm's thinking, a relationship of persons that involved intimacy and love. His letter abounds in expressions of such feelings. In fact, the language of intimacy and love are often extreme and overdone. At times, in reading the letters, one is forced to face the question: can he possibly feel that strongly about so many people? Even more puzzling is the strange phenomenon that he may write a very passionate letter to one monk and then at the close of the letter direct him to show it to another monk and tell him to accept it as if written directly to him. What are we to make of this? I would not want to question his sincerity. Could it be as simple as this: what he writes he can intend for both because they are all involved in a much bigger enterprise? They care for one another and love one another, because all of them are making their pilgrim way toward the heavenly city? On the way friends help one another speed up that pilgrim journey. Thus Anselm, perhaps with St. Paul's image of the race in mind, writes to a monk named Robert:

> When I see others running along easily on their way back to the heavenly home and myself, veritably weighed down by sins and lethargy, scarcely advancing on this path, I am forced by the realization of my great need to call out from the bottom of my heart to those ahead of me. Not that their speed should be slowed down by my sluggishness, but that my own slow pace, accelerated by the runners, should be made faster. (*Letters*, 1:79)

To be a friend, therefore, is to help a friend or to be helped by a friend. Thus friendship calls for mutuality. Such mutuality arises from a communion of wills in the service of God and is manifested in a shared solicitude: each concerned for the welfare of the other. But the object of this solicitude is principally spiritual and eternal. In other words, for Anselm the ultimate goal of friendship is eschatological. Time and time again he invites his friends to spiritual progress "so that with Christ's guidance you may reach the blessed company of the saints" (*Letters*, 1:77). Friendship grows and blossoms to the degree that each friend practices purity of heart and attaches himself or herself to God first and only then to the other — and to the other as he or she is in God.

An element of friendship that is important for Anselm is keeping one's friend in mind. This calls for reciprocal appreciation of the other, as well as a conscious awareness of him or her. Thus to his friend Gundulf he writes of their mutual awareness of one another.

You have my consciousness always with you. If you are silent,
I know that you love me; when I am silent you know that I
love you. You are conscious that I do not doubt you, and I
give witness to you that you are sure of me. We are then
conscious of each other's consciousness. Since we are conscious that we are in each other's minds, therefore, it only
remains for us to tell each other about our affairs so that we
may either rejoice together or be concerned for each other.
(my translation; see *Letters,* 1:4)

Such appreciation and awareness, it should be clear, are first
and foremost interior. That is why, though delight in the presence of the other can be viewed as an element of friendship,
still for friends, whose friendship is in God, absence in no way
effects a cooling of the ardor of their affection for one another.
Anselm, therefore, tends to minimize the importance of corpo-
ral presence. When it is the will of God that separates friends,
it is their very acceptance of God's will that unites them. For
it increases their likeness to one another in virtue. It might be
said that the *idem* of their friendship grows. Anselm expresses
this in a letter to a monk of Christchurch, Canterbury, whom
he had known at Bec. He writes:

To those whose minds the fire of love welds together, it is not
groundlessly irksome if the place they live keeps their bodies
apart. But since, whether we live or die, we are not our own
but the Lord's, we must direct our minds to what the Lord to
whom we belong wills to do with us, rather than to what we,
who do not belong to ourselves, want. (*Letters,* 1:84)

To his friend Gundulf he writes in a similar vein of the spiritual
ties that unite friends:

Both my Gundulf and your Anselm are witness that you and
I have no need whatever to declare our mutual affection to
each other by letter. Since your soul and my soul can never
bear to be absent from each other but are incessantly en-
twined together, nothing of ourselves is lacking to the other
except that we are not present to one another physically. But

why do I describe my love to you in a letter when you keep
the real image of it carefully in the ark of your heart? For
what is your love for me but the image of my love for you?
                                              (*Letters*, 1:144)

It isn't really a matter of "absence makes the heart grow
fonder," but rather that obedience to whatever is God's will for
us deepens our love not only for God but for our friend. Moreover, friends who by God's will are obliged to be absent from
one another can expect from God's love that they will be united
in the full communion of the saints. To Lanzo, a novice at Cluny,
Anselm writes: "When the pilgrimage of this life has come to
an end, with the help of the One toward whom we are traveling and in whom we place our hope, we shall come together
in that homeland toward which we are striving, as it were, by
different routes" (*Letters*, 1:133). This longing to be with one's
friend, with the realization that that longing will only be satisfied eschatologically, is a frequent theme in Anselm's letters.
To offer but one further instance, he writes to Arnulf, a monk
of Beauvais: "Your beloved love is precious to me, and although
we travel alone on this pilgrimage toward our heavenly home,
as by different paths, let us nevertheless pray for each other that
there we may eternally rejoice together in God" (*Letters*, 1:138).
    If it is correct to say that for Anselm the goal of the Chris-
tian life is to complete the pilgrim journey, in the company of
one's friends, to the heavenly city, and if it makes sense to say
that the saints are our heavenly friends who have already made
it and are rooting for us to join them, then I think I am on
safe ground when I assert that, in Anselm's mind, friendship
was closely related to the Christian belief in the communion of
saints. His letters make abundantly evident his belief that the
pleasure a person experiences in friendship on earth is a pale
reflection of the experience of friendship that continues in the
heavenly kingdom. He says as much in a letter to Ralph, who
was probably the prior at St. Stephen's monastery in Caen. He
speaks of their friendship and the fire of charity in each of them
that longs to be with the other. That longing which cannot be
fulfilled now, since God has willed that they travel by different
paths, will be abundantly satisfied in the heavenly city:

> As our life is short, so the day is near when we will be able to congratulate ourselves on nevermore being separated from [the Lord's] presence or each other's, if with his help we take care to pass through this short life agreeing with him in all things. In the meantime, however, whether the proximity of the places where we lie joins us or their distance separates us, let charity always make one spirit of the two of us.
>
> (*Letters*, 1:98–99)

Moreover, his prayers to the saints, which amount to lengthy conversations with these heavenly friends, and his intent that these prayers be used by others to increase their own fervor attest to the link he was eager to forge between those seeking the fullness of the holy life and those who have already attained it. He prays to the saints as his helpers. He asks St. John the Evangelist not to defend him, but to intercede for him with the One whom John relates to as beloved friend but whom Anselm fears as judge. He invokes Benedict, Nicholas, and Stephen as friends who are secure in their friendship with God. He begs them to ask for him what he dares not ask because of his unworthiness. Running through the prayers is the confidence he has: a confidence based not on his own merits, but on the love that he feels sure these heavenly friends are eager to extend to him. Anselm may dwell on his own sinfulness and his need to repent. They are the vicissitudes one must deal with on the way to salvation. Yet it's worth noting that his unworthiness never creates anxiety about the security of his faith. Despite stumbling at times, he never doubts that he is on the way. He has every confidence that he shall one day join the company of the heavenly hosts. Even in this mortal existence he is conscious of being in their company.

He would have enjoyed Father Meyendorff's story (which I received from Dr. Ross MacKenzie of the Chautauqua Institution). A visitor to a small church on a tiny island in the Aegean Sea asked the priest how many people usually worshiped in the little parish church on Sundays. The priest's answer was: "Oh, about ten to twelve thousand, I would suppose." The visitor was somewhat bewildered: "This is a tiny island," she said. "Where do all these people come from and how can they possibly fit into so small a church?" The priest smiled and then said to the visitor: "All the people who ever lived on this island since it received the Gospel message are still here. Just think of what we say in the sacred liturgy: 'Therefore with all the angels and saints and the whole company of the faithful we praise your glory forever.' Don't you realize," he added, "that when we sing the *trisagion* (the "Holy, Holy, Holy") we are joining with all the holy ones who have ever worshiped in this church?"

What an appropriate thought for Christian people to have in mind when they gather as a eucharistic community on the Lord's Day: many more are present and active in the celebration than mortal vision is able to see. Singing the "Holy, Holy, Holy" is our way of joining, even now, in the chorus of that heavenly company. It is even worth noting that it is not they who join us, but we who join with them.

The Prayer for Friends

Before considering Anselm's letters and the ways in which they manifest his relationship with friends, it will be worth our while to go back to the book of prayers and meditations to look at prayer 18: "The Prayer for Friends." In this prayer he struggles with a problem he must deal with and a command he must obey. The *problem* is his sinfulness, which would seem to prevent him from any effective prayer for his friends. The *command* is Jesus' command that we love one another, which surely suggests that we should pray for our friends. So what kind of friend would he be if he did not pray for his friends? Yet can the prayers of a sinner, such as he sees himself to be, actually be of any avail to his friends? He wrestles with this dilemma. Addressing himself to "sweet and gentle Lord Jesus Christ," he recalls the great love Jesus had shown, even to the point of praying for his executioners.

> You showed a love greater than anyone could possibly equal,
> for you in no way deserved death,
> yet you laid down your dear life for slaves and sinners.
> Indeed you prayed for your executioners,
> that you might justify them,

> make them your brothers,
> and reconcile them to your Father and to yourself.

In a mood of frustration he expresses his desire to do what Jesus commands, but that desire is clouded by the realization of his own sinfulness. Hardly able to ask pardon for himself, how can he ask pardon for his friends?

> O Lord, you who showed such great love to your enemies,
> have commanded that same love of your friends....
> Dear Lord, your servant wants, truly wants ever so much
> to pray for his friends,
> but standing accused before you,
> he is held back by the guilt of his own sins.
> Hardly able to ask pardon for myself,
> how dare I presume to ask it for others?

Yet he is not without hope. Obeying God brings with it a healing power. Loving others can itself wipe out the sins of the one who loves.

> [Yet] shall I ignore what you command,
> because I have done what you have forbidden?
> No! Since I presumed to do what was forbidden,
> I now embrace what is commanded,
> in the hope that obedience may heal my presumption
> and charity cover the multitude of my sins.
> Therefore, gracious and good God,
> I pray to you for those who love me on account of you
> and whom I love in you.
> With special devotion I pray
> for those whom you know love me
> and whom I most dearly love....
> And if my prayer does not deserve to help them,
> since it is offered to you by a sinner,
> may it avail for them,
> because it is done at your command....
> O Lord, my prayer lacks ardor,
> because my love lacks fervor.

> But, rich in mercy as you are,
> you will not measure your goodness to them
> by the coldness of my devotion;
> but as your goodness surpasses all human love,
> so may your readiness to hear
> transcend the tepidity of my prayer. (S. III, 71–72)

At this point we might want to pause a moment to reflect on our own prayers for our friends and what, if any, might be the obstacles to the fruitfulness of such prayers. As I have said earlier, Anselm sometimes overplays, even overdramatizes, his own sinfulness; yet, since we live in an age that deplores any talk about sin as morbid and unhealthy, it may be salutary for us to think about the ways in which our "falling short of the mark" (a good biblical understanding of sin) may cloud the value of the prayers we offer for one another. At the same time we must never forget that we are united with our friends in the community of love and with the Source of love that commands us to love.

The Prayer for Enemies

Jesus' love command embraces not only friends, but also enemies. In the sermon on the plain in Luke, Jesus tells us: "I say to you, love your enemies, do good to those who hate you ... " (Luke 6:27). With good reason, then, Anselm follows his prayer for friends with one for enemies:

> O Lord, you alone are powerful.
> You alone are merciful.
> Whatever you bid me desire for my enemies
> do give to them and give back to me.
> And should what I ask at any time for them
> be outside the rule of charity,
> because of ignorance, weakness, or malice,
> do not give this to them nor give it back to me.

It is worth noting, in the next part of the prayer, that Anselm seems to assume that those who are his enemies are people who

are in darkness or error; thus he prays that they may have light
and may find the truth:

> You are the true light;
> enlighten their darkness.
> You are the highest truth;
> correct their errors.
> You are the true life;
> give life to their souls.
> For you have said, through your beloved disciple,
> that he who loves not abides in death.
> Therefore, O Lord, I pray that you give them
> love for you and love for their neighbor,
> as you have commanded,
> lest they stand before you [guilty] of sin
> against their brother [or sister].

Yet he is conscious that his actions toward them might prove a
stumbling block that could lead them into sin.

> Most gentle Jesus, may I not be the occasion
> of death for my brothers [or sisters].
> May I not be a scandal or a stumbling block to them.
> My own sin is quite enough for me.
> Your servant implores for his fellow servants
> that they not offend the kindness
> of so great and good a Lord on my account.
> Let them be reconciled to you
> and in agreement with me
> according to your will and because of you. . . .
> Do this, my gracious creator and merciful judge
> according to your mercy that is without measure.
> Forgive me all my debts,
> as before you I forgive all my debtors. . . .
> Hear me, hear me, great and gentle Lord,
> my soul longs to feed itself
> on the experience of your love,
> but it cannot satisfy itself with you,
> for my mouth can find no name to call upon you

that will satisfy its longing....
I have prayed Lord as I am able,
but I wish I were more able.
Hear me, as you are able,
hear me, hear me, as you can,
for you can do all that you choose.
I pray as a weakling and a sinner;
hear me, you who are all powerful and all merciful.
I pray not just for my friends or enemies
[but also] that you distribute the healing power of your mercy
wherever you know it will help someone
who may not be in accord with your will,
whether he [or she] be living or dead.
And always hear me,
not as my heart wills or my mouth seeks,
but as you know and will that I ought to will and seek.
O savior of the world,
who lives and reigns with the Father and the Holy Spirit,
one God, forever and ever. Amen. (S. III, 73–75)

While Anselm's friends come from all ranks of society (he wrote to popes, kings, feudal lords, lay men and lay women), his most intimate letters are addressed to other monks.

Letter 112: To Hugh the Hermit

The warm letter of advice he wrote to Hugh the hermit is a typical example of a letter of friendship in which Anselm sets forth basic principles of spirituality. The letter was occasioned by Hugh's request for counsel about how to present the spiritual life to people who came to him seeking spiritual guidance. Pleading his own inadequacy, Anselm nonetheless responds because of his love for his friend. His letter is something of a summing up of Benedictine spirituality. It reflects, I believe, his own intimate union with God. The spirituality he describes mirrors the spirituality he lived.

Here is what he would say to people seeking advice about the spiritual journey (and since it is long I offer not a translation, but a brief paraphrase of it).

Dearest friend, God proclaims [the Latin is *clamat,* literally "shouts"] that he has the kingdom of heaven up for sale. What a wondrous kingdom it is! Human eye cannot see its splendor or the ear hear of it. Beyond all our powers of imagining, it is a place dominated by love: all loving God and one another, but God more than themselves.

This heavenly kingdom is the fulfillment of all human desires [a favorite Anselmian theme]. It is also, one might say, a fulfillment of what God desires for God's people. For in this kingdom all will accomplish God's will perfectly. This unity of wills, starting from each individual, spiraling out to embrace all persons, indeed all creation, finds fulfillment in the unity of all with God and in God.

Of course, there is a price tag for what God has put up for sale. True, there is nothing we can offer that will add to God's perfection; still God does not give so great a gift for nothing. And this is understandable, for no one would give something of great value to a person who fails to appreciate its value. God will give it only to those who love. When you think of it, the price isn't high at all. All God asks is love.

[Switching for a brief time to the second person, Anselm pleads:] Give love and receive the kingdom; love and possess. [Here is the heart of Anselm's spirituality expressed for once in an economy of words that highlights the intensity of his fervor:] Give love and get the kingdom. Love and it's all yours! Indeed if you love God more than yourself, you already have one foot in the heavenly kingdom. How can this be? Quite simply, for one who loves, heaven has already begun on earth. But [Anselm warns] there can be false love and true love. The kind of love that brings the gift of the kingdom requires purity of heart, nonattachment, emptying one's heart of all alien loves.

[Back once again to the third person, Anselm continues:] So it is that those who fill their hearts with love of God and their neighbor will nothing but what God wills or another person wills — as long as the latter is not contrary to what God wills.

[Anselm concludes with a brief admonition to devote oneself (a) to contemplation, (b) to active concern of those in need, and (c) to detachment from worldly goods.] It follows then that [those who do so] will desire God and will want with great eagerness to speak and hear and meditate about God whom they love so much. Those who wish to possess perfectly this love by which the kingdom of God is purchased will be concerned about the needs of others. They will be active in ministry: being compassionate toward those who mourn, rejoicing with those who rejoice, caring for the needy and unfortunate. Totally devoted to God and to others, they will no longer set any store on riches or power or being praised or honored. (See *Letters*, 1:268–71)

I don't suppose, good reader, that you have received any letters of quite this kind. How would you react to receiving one? Does this spirituality relate to you? Does it motivate you? It may be that the feudal image of the kingdom is somewhat foreign to your experience. But surely the basic call is familiar. It's the call of the Gospel which we have all heard. But what of the challenges Anselm issues: speaking to God, listening to God's word, meditating on God's presence? On the other hand, spirituality, as I have said earlier, cannot be reduced to exercises of prayer or meditation. Spirituality is life, lived in its totality. It is living our union with God and with our sisters and brothers. Yet spirituality needs nurturing. It can only grow in a person who has learned the value of quiet time in life when one can pray, meditate, just be in and with God. So, when Anselm calls us to speak with God, to listen to God's word, to meditate and be aware of God's presence, we need to listen. Some people are so busy that they will say with a sense of resigned helplessness: "I don't even have the time to think!" What they really mean is that they haven't the quiet time to think — or even just to be. They have, at great loss to themselves, failed to build silence into their lives. Our spirituality can manage to survive many trials and setbacks. It can scarcely survive in an atmosphere devoid of any silence.

Finally, a true spirituality, if it is to penetrate our lives, must include as a necessary ingredient a spirit of nonattachment: that form of spiritual maturity in which one no longer sets any store on those things that so many people seem to desire most: riches, power, honor, praise. How does one make such nonattachment a reality in a culture that is sophisticatedly geared to encourage just the opposite?

I remember Joan Chittister telling the story of a visitor who stopped at the home of a rabbi. Noting that the room was very sparsely furnished, he asked the rabbi: "Why don't you have more furniture?" The rabbi answered with a question: "Where is your furniture?" The visitor said: "Oh, I'm just passing through." "So am I," replied the rabbi. A culture in which having things and wanting more has become a way of life doesn't make it easy to remember that "we have here no lasting city, but we are seekers after the city which is to come" (Heb. 13:14).

Letter 59: To the Monk Gundulf

Gundulf, who had been a monk at Bec, was then brought to Canterbury by Lanfranc, and eventually was chosen bishop of Rochester, consistently complained that Anselm did not write to him often enough. In a letter sent sometime in 1076 Anselm reflects on the mystery of human friendship. Love between friends, written in the heart as it is, transcends the possibilities of words to express it. For, while friendship arises from the circumstances of our lives, it is not, in the first instance, of our own making, but a gift of God. Interestingly Anselm applies to friendship the words of St. Paul about the ineffability of the heavenly kingdom. That is why human friendship is a foretaste of the life of the blessed. It is a way of participating actively in the communion of saints. He says to Gundulf in effect: "You want me to put my love for you into words."

> But what of this, that neither eye has seen nor ear has heard,
> but only into the human heart has it entered —
> what affections loving hearts have laid up
> for those who love them.
> My witness is the experience of your own consciousness,
> that the taste of this affection is not perceived by any sight or hearing,
> except inasmuch as it is conceived in the mind of each.

Since [therefore you know this]. . . .
let our own consciousness suffice for us,
by which we are conscious to each other
of how much we love each other.[3]

Letter 434: To the Monk Walter

In a later letter written in 1106 to Walter, a monk of St. Wan-
drille at Fontenelle, Anselm points to the source of the mystery
of human love. It is nothing less than the Holy Spirit. It takes
on the character of a divine gift which can never be merited,
but only accepted with joy:

My soul wonders
whence your soul conceived such a great feeling of love for
   me—
unless it is that "the Spirit blows where it will,
and you hear its sound but you do not know
from where it comes or where it is going" (John 3:8).
Indeed my merits are unable to bring this about
with the Lord and with people, to make me so loved by
   anyone,
but the Holy Spirit, through whom charity is poured
into the hearts of the servants of God
has made your soul fruitful with so much and such great
   affection.
It is the Spirit's voice I hear in your letter
but know not whence he breathes it,
for I find in my soul no reason why he should do so.
I ask him never to depart from you,
but always to abide in you,
and to make your whole spirit burn unceasingly
with the love of God and of people. (*Letters,* 3:213)

Letter 35: To the Monk Herluin

Anselm writes to Herluin, a monk at Christchurch, Canterbury,
encouraging him to persevere faithfully in the monastic life. He

---

3. My translation: S. III, 173–74; see *Letters*, 1:171–72.

reminds Herluin of the fleeting character of mortal existence and calls on him to grow in virtue as time relentlessly moves on toward the end that will bring him eternal rest and a glorious crown in the company of the heavenly saints. Rest not in complacency, he warns; rather strive always to grow, even if this means reaching for spiritual goals never before attempted:

> It is true that the longer a person has lived,
> the shorter he has still to live;
> and the further he is from the day of his birth,
> the nearer he is to the day of his death
> and to the day of recompense for his whole life....
> Therefore the time for you to lead a good life grows shorter
>   every day.
> And so, dearly beloved, take care to use [well]
> the time which remains to you....
> The more you realize that your task
> is hastening toward the end
> and that you are approaching your rest and crown,
> the more you should progress
> by pressing on more resolutely,
> persevering more joyfully, courageously comforted.
> Do not abandon your undertaking by any lassitude, therefore,
> but rather for the love of blessed reward
> and in hope of divine assistance,
> embark on those things which are good for you
> and which you have not yet attempted,
> so that, with Christ's guidance,
> you may attain the blessed company of the saints.
>
> *(Letters,* 1:130–31)

Letter 34: To the Monk Gundulf

Friendship involves a belonging to one another. Anselm writes to Gundulf:

> Did I not know that I was everything to you
> and that you were everything to me?
> I would thank you for your gifts

> but since everything you have belongs to me
> and everything I have is yours,
> when you give me what belongs to you,
> why should I bow to you [in gratitude],
> when I am accepting not things belonging to somebody else
> but what are already mine? (*Letters,* 1:129)

Anselm is clearly using biblical language. In Luke 15:34, the father of the prodigal says to the elder son: "Son, you are always with me, and all that is mine is yours." The Fourth Gospel puts similar words on the lips of Jesus as he prays on behalf of his disciples: "All mine are yours and yours are mine" (17:10). There may also be here the sense of belongingness and something of Cicero's description of one's friend as *alter idem*.

Letters 165 and 178: To the Monks of Bec

It was at the abbey of Bec that Anselm found God. It was there that he came to understand his journey as a pilgrim toward the heavenly homeland. It is true to say, I think, that even after his reluctant acceptance of the archbishopric of Canterbury, his heart, or at least a good part of it, remained in Bec. His letters to the monks at Bec are the letters of a father speaking to the sons he loved. As a father he loves them with an affection that distance could never diminish. As a Benedictine father, he admonishes them to careful observance of the Holy Rule.

Soon after his consecration as archbishop of Canterbury (December 4, 1093), Anselm wrote to his beloved monks at Bec telling them of his joy that they have a new abbot. There is a poignancy in his rejoicing: he takes joy in God's will, even though it was not quite what he wanted. His hope had been that he would be able "to await with joy my life's end, and freed from every kind of earthly occupation, I might lead a quiet life in your midst." But he confesses that divine providence had other plans for him. Thus, he rejoices, on the one hand, that God had heard one of his prayers by giving his monks at Bec an abbot; on the other hand he grieves that God has not heard his prayer to be released from the earthly occupations that necessarily went along with being archbishop.

This letter is important for our understanding of Anselm. He reveals his reflective temperament, as he accepts the will of God in circumstances that do violence to that temperament. At the same time his paternal concern for the monks whom he had been forced to leave moves him to reflect with them about the spiritual life to which they have vowed themselves. He calls them to unity and mutual love and to obedience to their new abbot:

> Bearing paternal solicitude for you now as always,
> I admonish you as my dearest sons,
> as those whom I loved
> and wish to continue to love with most tender affection
> in the compassion of Christ,
> be of one mind toward one another,
> according to the holy Apostle [Rom. 12:16].
> May you daily direct the intention of your souls toward better
> things,
> and show humble obedience toward him
> whom divine loving kindness wished to place over you.
>
> (*Letters,* 2:57–58)

Anselm also addresses himself to William, the new abbot. In his words of advice we glean an understanding of what Anselm thought an abbot should be. William is admonished to be watchful of the souls of the brothers who are under obedience to him. This will enable them to rejoice in having found the shelter of a good shepherd. He calls on William to exercise the moderation that St. Benedict so clearly calls for in the Rule.

> May you hasten to prove yourself
> moderate in everything you do,
> so that kindness does not exclude justice nor justice exclude
> kindness. . . .
> May you combine the one with the other, so that by means
> of both
> good order may be preserved in the monastery
> with spotless uprightness of conduct.

He concludes his letter with a plea for the continued love and affection of the monks of Bec: "Do not allow the love of your kindness for me to cool down, because even though I cannot be present to you in body, yet through the love of my heart for you, I never cease to be with you." Finally, he encourages them to hospitality, to gain friends for the monastery. "Never," he says, "think that you have enough friends." Clearly for him friendship is a means of ascent to God. The more friends a monastery has the more people it can help to reach the heavenly homeland.

The heart-warming letter 178, directed to the same monks some months after Anselm had been installed as archbishop of Canterbury, carries the salutation: "to his most loved and most longed-for friends, Abbot William and the other servants of God living in the monastery of Bec, Brother Anselm, by profession and still in his heart a monk of Bec, though by God's will called to be archbishop of Canterbury."

He is grateful to them for their fraternal charity toward him, set aflame as it is by loving compassion, as they pray divine help for him in the troubles he is experiencing with the king. But there is really no need for him to express this gratitude, so deeply enshrined in his heart, for "where there is so great a unity of hearts and souls, our awareness of one another's feelings is greater than tongue or pen could possibly express."

His most important message for them is that, wherever his body may be, his soul is ever theirs. He sorely misses them. It is only his contemplation of, and submission to, the will of God that enables him to bear so great a loss. Yet it does give him joy to write them in order to encourage and stimulate their advance along the road to perfection. That road is marked out from them by the Holy Rule. Hence the body of the letter is something of a summary of the spirit of the Rule of St. Benedict, especially Rules 2 and 5:

> But that you may be able to bring about [this advance in holiness] more efficaciously,
> watch over, admonish, correct one another in a spirit of charity,
> and accept whatever corrections you receive
> from one another as great gifts bestowed upon you.

Let superiors be kind to their subjects so as to sustain them
    in fervor.
May they inflame with enthusiasm those who are slothful
and chastise with proper discipline those who are rebellious.
Those of you who are subjects, submit to your superiors
and especially to the abbot with unfeigned obedience.
Be dutiful subjects, not reluctant ones.
For subjects sin greatly before God
if they are unconcerned about being a burden to their
    superiors,
who have undertaken,
only through fear of God and out of fraternal charity,
to carry them [as their burden].[4]

Anselm continues to exhort them to fulfillment of the Rule. He
stresses the importance of the vow of stability: they should not
be away from the monastery unless obedience requires it. Those
who leave the enclosure without proper reason do harm not
only to themselves but to the community: they become occa-
sions of murmuring among the other monks. He calls them also
to hospitality: they are to receive guests with joy and minister
to them cheerfully.

Is This Advice for Us?

In this letter to the monks at Bec, Anselm shows, as he did in
the previous letter, the high value he places on mutual love of
the brothers one for another and on obedience to superiors. He
writes to a community formed by the Rule of St. Benedict: a rule
that has built and sustained monastic communities for some fifteen hundred years and continues to do so today. What might
Anselm have to say today, if he were writing, not so much to
monks, but to any community of people in today's world?

Think of the communities we belong to: family, church, religious community, the national and international communities,
indeed, any group united in its commitment to a common goal.

---

4. My translation: S. IV, 61–62; see *Letters*, 2:93–94.

Would his simple advice given to the monks of Bec and based on the Rule of St. Benedict be helpful to us? Notice that he calls for three things that he believes will enhance community: (1) love for one another, (2) obedience to superiors, and (3) hospitality.

The first and most essential ingredient of good community is mutual love. Can anyone doubt that such love and concern of members for the well-being of one another would indeed improve the quality of any community? If we can readily accept his first requirement for community, we may not accept the second (obedience) with equal readiness.

At first hearing obedience may pose difficulties, especially in communities where those in authority attempt to manipulate the community and its resources for their own personal gain. Yet if we realize that obedience, in its etymology (*ob* + *audire*), means a willingness to listen, some of the difficulties may disappear. It is possible to translate Anselm's call for obedience into a request for a willing readiness to enter into dialogue about the affairs of the community. People who are able to talk to one another are people who learn from one another. Yet dialogue is never an end in itself: no community can survive on dialogue that never reaches a conclusion or never adopts a course of action. After all the dialogue has taken place, someone must be able to articulate the mind of the community and expect the assent and cooperation of the community's members. This is to say that there must be a leader in the community who has the authority finally to say: "This is what we believe. This is what we choose to do."

Finally, Anselm's call to hospitality may, in some situations at least, be threatening to people in our present-day culture. People are wary of strangers. To welcome the stranger as Christ (which Benedict calls for) might be seen as naïve and perhaps even dangerous. We live in a culture wherein a handout may be viewed as easier (and safer) than a welcome. In such a context hospitality may demand of us a significant change in attitudes.

It is also possible to view hospitality in a wider dimension: to see it as a challenge to set aside prejudice, to accept people as they are and at the same time to help them become what they can be. Hospitality is especially an invitation to care for the needs of the poor, the homeless, the hungry, the imprisoned, and all those who are victimized by a society that so easily values people in terms of their means rather than their meaning. At its deepest roots hospitality demands that we value persons in terms of their God-given meaning, namely, that inalienable dignity and worth persons have simply as persons.

Hospitality can also take on ecological significance, namely, a respect for the meaning of the good earth that God has given us with the charge to be good stewards. This can involve obedience too, namely, listening to God speaking to us through nature. Reverencing God's great gift of creation demands that we refuse to misuse, to desecrate, to pollute the environment in which we live. There is a lovely "ecological" hymn about "hospitality to the earth" called "Stewards of Earth," which is sung to the melody of Jean Sibelius's "Finlandia." I quote the first and third verses.

> All praise to you, O Lord of all creation;
> You made the world and it is yours alone.
> The planet earth you spun in its location,
> Amid the stars adorning heaven's dome.
> We lease the earth but for a life's duration.
> Yet for this life it is our cherished home.
>
> To tend the earth is our entrusted duty.
> For earth is ours to use and not abuse.
> O gracious Lord, true source of all resources,
> Forgive our greed that wields destruction's sword.
> Then let us serve as wise and faithful stewards
> While earth gives glory to creation's Lord.

The Rule of St. Benedict came into existence at a time when extreme asceticism had become the honored way to achieve holiness of life. The more you could mortify the flesh, the holier you would become. Benedict saw the danger in such an understanding of the way to the holy life: it isolated a particular practice and carried it to extremes. It lost sight of the fact that spirituality is about living as a full human being totally devoted to God and to God's people. Measuring one's spirituality by the degree of mortification one "indulges in" is, quite simply, to set false priorities.

Aware of this danger, Benedict made sure, therefore, that the Rule he wrote was characterized by moderation. Moderation, however, should not be confused with mediocrity. The Rule makes demands on those who wish to live by it, yet, because those who came to live the monastic life differed widely in age, ability, and character, Benedict wisely tailored these demands to the needs and personalities of individual communities. Joan Chittister, in her fine commentary on the Rule of St. Benedict, shows how readily Benedict was willing to adapt the requirements of the Rule, though without mitigating them. It may well be that this insistence on moderation and this willingness to adapt (not compromise) explain why the Rule of St. Benedict has endured for centuries as a source of life and growth for so many thousands of people in many different places and in the context of very diverse cultures.

Rule 49 has to do with the observance of Lent in the monastery. The Rule proposes a very high ideal: the life of a monk should be a life of continuous Lent. But, since few have the strength to do this, monks are encouraged to do something extra in the way of prayer and abstinence during Lent. But (once again the modification that respects individual differences and also puts a brake on those whose zeal might lead them to go to excesses beyond their endurance) everyone needs to make known to the abbot what he intends to do. "Whatever is undertaken without the permission of the spiritual father will be reckoned as presumption and vainglory, not deserving a reward."

In letter 196 Anselm writes to Richard, a monk at Bec, urging him to moderate his fasting in obedience to Anselm himself and to Richard's abbot.

I fear that, while in your heart you wish to obtain a reward,
or rather gain a reputation or empty prestige through fasting,
you are more likely to incur punishment for your
    disobedience.
Certainly, just as simple obedience
merits a more valuable crown

than abstinence from food beyond the common practice,
so whoever scorns the first will be more severely punished
than he who forsakes the second.
Obedience can save a person without this sort of fasting;
without obedience such fasting can only lead to damnation.
(Letters, 2:128)

Anselm pleads with Richard to practice the moderation which both Anselm himself and the abbot of Bec have prescribed. "It is quite true," Anselm writes, "that your body and your character cannot tolerate what your imprudence presumes to do." Finally, he admonishes Richard that if he wishes to show his love for Anselm and retain Anselm's love, he will abandon his immoderate and vainglorious practice and listen to the direction of his abbot. And this means listening to the Rule by which he has vowed to live his life: a rule that is always on the side of prudence and common sense.

In letter 285 (*Letters*, 2:194–96) Anselm replies to a request of Conus, a monk from Arras. Conus had heard Anselm speak about the three kinds of pride, but he could only remember one. He begs Anselm to refresh his memory. Anselm's reply is an interesting example of his moral theology. It makes clear that for him the essence of moral responsibility is in the will, in the intention. Here are his three degrees of pride:

1. Pride in judgment, when a person *thinks* more highly of himself than he ought.

2. Pride in the will, when a person *wants* to be treated differently and more highly than he has a right to.

3. Pride in action, when a person *treats* himself more highly than he ought.

Of the three the lightest, in terms of responsibility, is the third: it is based on ignorance and it can be cured. The one for which responsibility is greatest is the second, pride in the will. It is the most culpable of the three, because the person sins consciously. He or she intends the prideful action. Moral evil is primarily in the evil intention. The first is in some ways the most problematic, for it cannot be cured, precisely because the person has made an erroneous judgment and is not conscious that he or she is guilty of pride. The action is objectively wrong, but not intended.

This brief letter, coupled with the eschatological bent of Anselm's thinking, is a kind of introduction to basic principles of a moral theology that is strikingly familiar to us. In our own day Bernard Häring, in his monumental breakthrough in moral theology entitled *The Law of Christ,* suggests two virtues essential for the good moral life: vigilance and responsibility. Anselm's emphasis on eschatology and on the importance of the moral intention would fit well with Häring's perceptions on moral issues.

During his tenure as primate of England, Wales, and Ireland, Anselm wrote to Muirchertach, the king of Ireland, congratulating him for letting the people of his realm live in peace. Such peace creates an atmosphere in a country that makes for the achievement of much good. "Where there is peace it is possible for people of good will to accomplish what they choose." But, unfortunately, not all in his realm are people of good will. Anselm, ever so gently, invites the king to "consider whether there are any things in your kingdom which have to be corrected for the sake of eternal life." Anselm knows that such things do exist. Before mentioning what he has in mind, he admonishes the king: "Nothing that can be corrected should be neglected." God holds us responsible, he warns the king, not only for what we do wrong, but also for failing to correct the wrongs which we are able to correct. Such responsibility weighs especially heavy on those who are in positions of power.

Having laid down some fundamental moral principles, Anselm moves to practical cases. Marriages in Ireland, as he has heard, are being dissolved without sufficient grounds. Relatives are intermarrying despite canonical impediments. Bishops are being consecrated by one bishop alone, whereas there should be three bishop-consecrators.

Anselm advises the king to take counsel with wise men in his realm and deal with these and other matters that may need correction. But Anselm is a realist. Deep-seated wrongs that are of long standing cannot be easily and quickly undone. He admonishes the king to do what he can; at the same time he suggests patience and perseverance. "If, however, you cannot do everything at once, you should not for that reason give up trying to progress from better things to even better ones. For God usually perfects good intentions and good efforts with kindness and repays them with abundance" (*Letters*, 3:203).

This advice — to move from where we are at the moment to where we can go now — is a good principle not only for dealing with the needs of the social order, but also for making spiritual progress. We don't become saints all at once. Traveling toward the heavenly city calls for listening to the voice of God (and sometimes we don't always hear very well) and accepting the grace of the present moment. Friends can encourage one another to listen more carefully to what God may be saying to us. Friends can help us to see the moment of grace that without them we might miss. For friends are people who share many things. What they especially share is the pilgrim desire to journey together to the heavenly city. My friend is someone who wants me to become better than I am and who helps me to do so. Friendship, therefore, is one of God's greatest gifts to us. Anselm's letters amply illustrate how much he appreciated the gift of friendship.

Texts for Reflection

The longer someone has lived, the shorter he [she] has still to live; and the farther he [she] is from the day of birth, the nearer to the day of death. (*Letters*, 1:77)

❖

You cannot be everywhere where you are loved, but you can be loved and good wherever you may be. (*Letters*, 1:192)

❖

Since in the exile of this life I am enjoined never to cease encouraging all whom I can to progress toward the heavenly homeland, certainly I ought not withhold this service from those to whom I know I am joined by the debt of love. (*Letters*, 2:96)

If for God's sake, we ought to love our enemies in order to please God, much more ought we to love our friends in order not to displease God. (*Letters,* 2:220)

No one who acts rightly wishes to live for himself alone. But just as he desires and believes that, if he is a member of God, all the advantages of the other members will be his in the life to come; so in the same way, if there is any good in him, he ought to wish that it should belong to others in this life. (*Letters,* 3:74)

We should always strive more to love than to be loved, and to rejoice more, realizing that we gain more when we love than when we are loved. (*Letters,* 3:213)

❖

Wherever you are, either in the sight of people or only in the sight of God, from whom you are never separated, in all your actions, great or small, even in your thoughts, always with the psalmist carry your souls in your hands. May almighty God so protect you and direct you that God may lead you through temporal good fortune toward eternal happiness. (*Letters,* 3:303)

Chapter 4

Christ and Redemption

Anselm develops a soteriology that implies and suggests a profoundly contemplative view of God's plan for man and for the cosmos.   — THOMAS MERTON

Anselm deduced the necessity of the Incarnation from the nature of God and the need to protect the rational beauty of the universe which He had created.   — R. W. SOUTHERN

My friend Michael, now a young man of twenty-two, was at the age of two a precocious child, with perspectives appropriate to his age. On one occasion a couple of weeks into Lent, Michael asked his mother, Phyllis: "Has Jesus died yet?" His question was not theological, but pragmatic, in intent. He was looking forward to Easter and candy and other sweets that he knew came with the feast. But he also knew that before Easter's joys could become available, Jesus had to die. The necessity of Jesus' death, a practical issue for Michael (though he wasn't quite sure why), has been a theological issue for the Christian church from its very beginning.

Why was it necessary for Jesus to die? What role does his death play in our regard? In fact, we can go back one step further: why Jesus in the first place? Why did God choose in Jesus Christ to enter into the human situation? Why did God become incarnate? Or, to use Anselm's title for one of his most important works: *Cur Deus Homo* (hereafter CDH).

The title *Cur Deus Homo* is difficult to translate. To have it mean: "Why God became Man" is to risk the accusation of sexist exclusivism. To translate it: "Why God became human" seems to weaken the statement by substituting an adjective for a noun. There is also the question: Does Anselm mean "Homo" to indicate a human being or humanity in general? The whole tone of the book suggests that he intended a particular human being. It may well be that the best we can do is to read Anselm's words in this way: "Why God became a human being."

The question of the meaning and necessity of the Incarnation was something that sooner or later Anselm was bound to deal with for the simple reason that questions about the Incarnation lie at the heart of the Christian mystery. As R. W. Southern has written: "Without a consideration of the Incarnation his theology would have remained essentially incomplete: the theology of a Christian God unattached to the Christian dispensation."[1]

The *Cur Deus Homo*

The CDH was a product of Anselm's later years and was produced in a context very different from that out of which his earlier writings had come. The earlier writings came into being at the request of his monks. They had listened with joy to the many talks he had given them and eagerly awaited his putting his words to manuscript. His topics too, in those earlier writings, were of his own choosing, namely, God: the divine existence and perfection; and prayer and meditation: the source of strength and light to guide people on their pilgrim journey to the heavenly homeland. And there were the letters of his years while at Bec, the time before he became archbishop of Canterbury. For the most part these were expressions of affection and bits of spiritual counsel for those whom he hoped to help as he traveled with them in their mutual journey along the pilgrim way to life's final destination.

In his later years, what may well be considered his greatest work, certainly his most significant in terms of its influence on later theological thought, was produced in a less congenial atmosphere and under more difficult and distracting circumstances. The CDH was written over a period of years: begun when he was in England, worked on intermittently between 1094 and 1097, finally completed in 1098 when Anselm was in

---

1. *St. Anselm and His Biographer*, 81.

exile and staying at Liberi in the province of Capua in southern Italy. The work is cast in the form of a dialogue between Anselm and Boso. Boso was representative of the young monks who had listened to Anselm at Bec. Anselm was fond of him and asked the abbot of Bec to allow Boso to be with him as a dialogue partner and sometimes critic in the writing of CDH.

Anselm's Preface

Anselm was clearly upset when he learned that his manuscript of the CDH had been transcribed by others when it was still incomplete and not fully representative of his thinking. For this reason, he wrote a preface and directed that it be placed at the beginning of any copies of CDH. He makes clear that he had hastened to complete this work — and therefore wrote more quickly and more briefly than he would have wanted — because of his concern that incomplete copies of this work that were already in circulation were open to serious misinterpretation of his thinking.

> Had an undisturbed and adequate time been allowed me for finishing it, I should have introduced and added a number of things about which I was [forced to be] silent. It was with great anguish of heart (the reasons for which only God understands) that at the entreaty of others I began this work in England and completed it as an exile in the province of Capua. (S. II, i, 42)

When Anselm wrote this preface he could not have known that his explanation of atonement would become an important part of the Christian tradition that would be handed down to later generations, and that in the process of that handing down would be severely, even brutally, misinterpreted. All too frequently the doctrine of atonement has pictured an angry God demanding that the divine justice be satisfied. Adequate satisfaction could be achieved only through the shedding of blood. This presentation of the doctrine of atonement has all too often been ascribed to Anselm. It is something he would have strongly repudiated.

To return once again to the preface, Anselm points out that the CDH is divided into two books.

The first book contains the objections of unbelievers
who disdain the faith of Christians which they consider
    contrary to reason;
it [includes also] the replies of Christians [to these
    objections].
At the same time it proves by necessary reasons
that, leaving Christ aside [*remoto Christo*],
as if nothing were known about him,
it is impossible for anyone to be saved without him.
In the second book, again as if nothing were known about
    Christ,
it is shown by plain and simple reasoning
that every human being was created
to enjoy one day a blessed immortality in both body and
    soul.
It shows further that it was necessary
for humans to attain the end for which they were created
and that this [cannot be achieved]
except through one who is divine and human.
Thus [this second book] shows that
all we believe about Christ must necessarily take place.

(S. II, i, 42)

Subject and Occasion

In the first chapter Anselm makes clear the subject of the book and what occasioned it. As in the case of his earlier works, such as the *Monologion,* eager inquirers had invited him, by word and by letter, to put into writing what he had discoursed about with some of them concerning the mystery of the Incarnation. The book arose, therefore, out of their request that he give them reasons why it was necessary that God become human and suffer death in order to restore life to the world. It was not that these inquirers needed to have their faith justified; what they sought was the deeper joy that would come from understanding more clearly what they earnestly believed. As Anselm put it:

> What they were seeking was not
> that they might attain to faith through reason
> [for indeed they had faith],
> but that they might take delight
> in the understanding and contemplation
> of what they already believed.
> Yet another thing they sought,
> namely, that they might be prepared, as far as possible,
> to give a satisfactory answer to those [unbelievers]
> who demanded of them a reason for the hope that is in us.
>
> (S. II, i, 47)

Anselm indicates that it was Boso more than any other who convinced him to write this book. An interesting trip through the CDH is to read the parts "assigned" to Boso. At times he seems to be little more than a straight man for Anselm. Practically every possible way of expressing approval of another's statements is put on the lips of Boso. "We ought to acknowledge this." "There is no doubt of this." "It is so." "Nothing is more true." "What you say is reasonable." "I cannot deny it." "I must agree with you." "You have relieved my objection." "I do not see how this can be denied." "This is most plain." "I cannot help seeing this."

But Boso is more than a straight man: he is a young monk searching for answers, a willing partner in dialogue, a critic who persists in wanting satisfactory answers. He puts to Anselm the fundamental question that will constitute the substance of the CDH: Why did the omnipotent God assume our weak human nature to restore what sin had lost? When Anselm protests that he is not equal to the task, Boso refuses to be put off. He reminds Anselm that, in discussing a particular question, it often happens that God will help us to see what hitherto had been concealed. A thoughtful reminder to Anselm and indeed to all of us that, where there is sincere and open dialogue, God can become a third party shedding light where before there had been darkness or ambiguity.

Anselm accepts Boso's invitation and makes clear his desire to enter into dialogue with him and with those whom he may be said to represent.

Since I see your eagerness and that of others
who with you are motivated by love and by religious zeal
to seek some answers [to their questions],
I will try—to the best of my ability
and with the help of God and your prayers
(which you have often promised me)—
not so much to make clear the things you inquire about
as to inquire about them with you. (S. II, i, 50)

Boso also suggests the direction the book should take. You are not writing for intellectuals, he tells Anselm, but for people like me. "What I am asking of you, you will be writing not for the learned but for me and for those who are seeking this solution together with me" (CDH, c. 1). Who are those others? They may well have been other monks who, like Boso, were seeking a deeper understanding of what they believed. But these "others" also include unbelievers. Boso tells Anselm:

It is proper for us when we seek to investigate
the reasonableness of our faith
to propose the objections of those
who are wholly unwilling to submit to the same faith,
without the support of reason.
For although they appeal to reason because they do not believe,
we, on the other hand, [do so] because we do believe,
nevertheless the thing sought is one and the same. (S. II, i, 50)

The "unbelievers" included the Jews, but also the Muslims; for the objections of Jews and Muslims against Christian belief in the Incarnation would have been much the same. In their view it does dishonor to God, "when we affirm that God descended into the womb of a virgin, was born of woman,...that God endured fatigue, hunger, thirst, blows, and crucifixion and death among thieves" (S. II, i, 50). There is no evidence suggesting that Anselm ever actually discussed such matters with any Jews or Muslims. Eadmer, though, offers an interesting insight which suggests that, when writing with Muslims in mind, Anselm was not belaboring some imaginary Muslim. For he tells us that, while Anselm was at Capua (where he completed the

CDH), Roger, count of Sicily, was there with his army, which had a large Arab contingent. Eadmer remarks how Anselm "received all without any acceptance of persons. . . . They [the Muslims] gratefully accepted offerings of food from Anselm and returned to their own people making known the wonderful kindness they had experienced at his hands" (*Vita Anselmi*, 112). He tells also how, when Anselm passed through their camp, they called blessings upon him and reverenced him for his kindness and liberality. Anselm's "popularity" among these Muslim soldiers suggests something of an ecumenical attitude on his part in an age that was decidedly unecumenical.

A New Direction in Understanding Atonement

In the CDH Anselm departs in a significant way from the tradition that had come down to him from the patristic writers in general and from St. Augustine in particular. He rejects the long-held theory that Jesus' death ransomed humanity from the dominion of the Devil. According to this theory, when Adam yielded to the temptations of the Devil, he sold himself and all humanity into slavery to the Devil. The Devil's dominion, brought about by the voluntary submission of humans to him, gave the Devil certain rights which not even the omnipotence of God could breach without doing an injustice to the Devil. Atonement for sin, therefore, was a struggle between God and the Devil, fought on a cosmic battlefield, with humans cast in the role of silent bystanders. God won, because, as Southern puts it, "God was the master-strategist."[2] God became human. The Devil, failing to see the divinity in incarnate God, claimed authority over this divine-human being and put him to death. Having put the Innocent One to death, the Devil clearly had overstepped his rights and thus lost his dominion over humanity. The Incarnation was the divine strategy that won back for humans the possibility of once again achieving heavenly beatitude. It is this explanation of redemption that Anselm totally rejects:

---

2. *The Making of the Middle Ages*, 235.

I fail to see the force of the argument
we customarily make use of, namely,
that the Devil, by putting to death One
who did not deserve death and who was God,
justly lost his power over sinners.
[No! Anselm would say:
the Devil never had any rights over humans in the first place!]
If he had, it would have been unjust of God to make humans
    free,
since [in the argument of the tradition]
they had voluntarily and without coercion
given themselves over to the Devil's dominion.
                    (S. II, i, 56–57 freely translated and simplified)

For such a theory Anselm had nothing but contempt. It did not square with his firm understanding of the absolute sovereignty of God. Southern puts it well:

He had too uncompromising and too unitary a view of God's dominion over the whole creation to accept any view which allowed the Devil, or any other rebel, a claim to justice against God. Rebellion deserved nothing but punishment and to have seduced mankind into rebellion only increased the punishment: it did not create an Empire.[3]

With the Devil thus moved off the stage of the drama of redemption, there remained only God and humans confronting one another. For Anselm humans, deep in sin, were powerless to repair the harm their sin had done. Yet humans could be saved by God in a most fitting way through the Incarnation, whereby a divine-human being atones for sin and makes humanity into a new creation.

Interestingly, at the very time Anselm was developing his understanding of the way salvation was achieved, a new appreciation of the humanity of Christ was entering the patterns of medieval thought. Increasingly in Christian art, the Great

---

3. *St. Anselm and His Biographer,* 95.

Judge, the Pantocrator, was yielding place to the suffering Savior. Southern describes the new landscape of Christian faith: "The figure on the cross was seen with a new clarity to be that of a Man. The Devil slipped out of the drama and left God and Man face to face."[4]

In chapter 7 of book 1 of the CDH, where Anselm formulates his rejection of the theory that the Devil had acquired rights over humanity, he makes an interesting point which suggests his personal commitment to nonviolence. He suggests that those who believe in the Devil's rights over humans are led astray by the fact that they see humans "justly exposed" to the tormenting of the Devil. Anselm even concedes that God permits this. But, he goes on to argue, "the very same thing, seen from opposite points of view, can sometimes be both just and unjust." Thus, the Devil may appear to be tormenting people justly because God permits it. But this does not mean that the Devil is therefore an instrument of God and thus actually does punish justly. Anselm offers an insightful analogy in which he enunciates a clear principle of nonviolence:

> Suppose that someone strikes an innocent person unjustly;
> then the assailant justly deserves to be beaten himself.
> If however the innocent party,
> though he ought not to avenge himself,
> [actually does so] by beating his assailant,
> he acts unjustly. (S. II, i, 57)

"He ought not to avenge himself and if he does so he acts unjustly" — this is a reprise of the Gospel and also of the Rule of St. Benedict. This is what Mohandas Gandhi and Dorothy Day and Thomas Merton discovered in the Gospels. A disciple of Jesus is committed to a nonviolent way of life. These words on nonviolence are a bit of an aside, but still helpful in adding to our understanding of Anselm.

Having pointed out a traditional approach which Anselm rejected, I want to express in more detail his understanding of atonement. The argumentation in the CDH is complex; it

---

4. *The Making of the Middle Ages*, 236.

therefore calls for careful reading from anyone who hopes to understand it. And indeed not only careful reading but also prayerful reflection. Near the end of chapter 9 in book 2, Boso says: "The way by which you are leading me is so well defended by reason that I cannot deviate from it to the right or to the left" (S. II, ii, 106). In response Anselm speaks of the importance of being enabled by the grace of God to come to an understanding of truth. "It is not I who lead you," he says, "but the One of whom we are speaking, without whose guidance we have no power to keep to the way of truth" (S. II, ii, 106). The best theology, he is telling us, is that which is done in an atmosphere of prayerful openness to God and to the presence of divine grace.

Given the complex nature of the CDH, it may be well, as a first approach to its reasoning, to express its major elements in simple form before discussing some of it in greater detail.

The Divine Plan (Paradise): God created human beings for eternal happiness and placed them in a universe where there was order and beauty.

Human Sin (Paradise Lost): Human waywardness thwarted the divine plan and threw the whole universe into disorder. Sin, which may be defined as not giving God what is due to God, dishonors God. It places humans in a state of indebtedness from which they cannot recover. The order of the universe is disrupted; the beauty of creation is defaced. Humans long for deliverance from sin, but are unable by themselves to achieve that deliverance.

The Problem: God cannot allow the divine plan to be frustrated forever. Therefore the guilt of human sin must be taken away. The original blessing given to humanity, which humans cannot recover, nevertheless must be recovered. The order of the universe must be restored, its beauty reclaimed. In a word, satisfaction must be made for sin. Humans must pay the debt they owe to God. But this poses a twofold problem:

(a) a human being ought to pay the debt, because a human being contracted it. But clearly no human being is able to pay the debt, because humanity has nothing to give that has not been received from God nor can humanity pay anything that is worthy of God.

(b) God can pay the debt (or even remit it) but God ought not do so, because the debt is not God's; it is a human debt.

The Solution (Paradise Regained): Since humanity must provide the satisfaction, but only God can provide it, the solution to what appears an unsolvable problem is that satisfaction be offered by one who is both human and divine. Therefore God chooses to become human in Christ. Through the perfect obedience of Christ unto death — an obedience freely given out of love — satisfaction is rendered, God's honor is restored, in Christ humanity is saved, the order and beauty of the universe are regained. Humanity united in Christ — the divine-human being — can achieve the eternal life God intended from the beginning. The human longing for deliverance from sin is satisfied.

The Wonder of Divine Wisdom and Love: The Incarnation expresses in a wonderful way the divine wisdom: human salvation is made possible in a way that befits God (because it is achieved by One who is truly God) and makes human participation in the saving action a reality (since Incarnation means that the One who pays the debt is human as well as divine). The Incarnation also witnesses to God's love: Humans are not abandoned by God. Instead God's love triumphs over human waywardness.

In the light of these insights, derived solely from human reason, Anselm believes, a person who knows nothing about Christ (*remoto Christo*) can come to understand the necessity of the Incarnation. I should perhaps point out that in reading Anselm one has to deal somewhat gingerly with the term "necessary argument." Whether he is talking about the Incarnation (as in the CDH) or the Trinity (as in the *Monologion* and the *Proslogion*) his rational explanations of such Christian beliefs do not imply that human persons can penetrate the deep truths of faith without God's help. They are not philosophical demonstrations that operate independently of prior faith. He does believe, however, that they would be appealing to any person who reads them with an open mind and a righteous will. "Necessity" for him means what makes sense, what is appropriate and fitting. Thus, when he uses the term "necessity" in the CDH, he is talking not only about what is "logically necessary," but also what is "most fitting." Anselm speaks rather sternly to Boso about this matter: "I want it to be perfectly understood between us that we do not allow anything even the least unbecoming to be ascribed to God" (S. II, i, 67). God always *does* and *must* do what is most fitting. There cannot be the slightest deficiency in God or in God's creation. "[This principle] exhibited the perfection of God in a new light: everything that God does follows a perfect order that is not only perfect in its rationality, but also supremely beautiful."[5]

Boso's Questions and Anselm's Responses

One way of discussing the details of the CDH is to make use of some of the questions Boso put to Anselm in the course of their dialogue. Here are three basic questions he poses together with Anselm's replies.

Question 1: The Humiliation of the Incarnation

How can it be reasonably proved that God ought to or even could have condescended to such humiliation as the Incarnation entails? (see II, i, 51–52).

Anselm responds: Does not the reason God ought to do what we say God has done become understandable to the human mind, [when we consider] (*a*) that the human race, a most precious creation of God, would otherwise have perished, (*b*) how unfitting it would be that God's plans for humanity end up in ruin, and (*c*) that God's purposes for the human race could not be achieved unless the human race was delivered by its Creator? (see II, i, 52). This could be summed up: Humans are precious to God. God has plans for them. These plans cannot be allowed to fail. Only God can keep them from failing. The Incarnation shows the lengths to which God's love will go: God will embrace the human condition in order to save humans and preserve the order and beauty of creation.

---

5. Southern, *St. Anselm: A Portrait in a Landscape*, 181.

Question 2: The Possibility of a Sinless Being

Why didn't God create a new sinless human being who could then satisfy for human sinfulness?

Anselm's response: Don't you realize that, if a sinless human being were to liberate humanity from eternal death, humans would rightly become the servants of that sinless being? Were this to happen, humans would not be restored to the dignity that would have been theirs had they never sinned. For, though destined to be God's servants for all eternity and equals of the holy angels, they would now be servants of a being who was not God and whom the angels did not serve.

> If God made a new man, not of Adam's race,
> then this man would not belong to the human family
> which was born of Adam.
> Hence he ought not to make atonement
> for a family to which he did not belong.
> For it is right that a human should make atonement
> for the fault of a human,
> but it should be that human himself [or herself]
> or someone of the same family.
> Otherwise neither Adam nor anyone of his race
> would be making atonement. (S. II, ii, 102–3)

Question 3: The Possibility of Simple Forgiveness

Why didn't God simply forgive human sin? Why was the Incarnation necessary? If God created the universe by a single word, why could God not have redeemed humans by a simple act of the divine will rather than through the action of the divine-human being? Would it not be a denial of God's power if he did not do this or of his wisdom if he chose not to do it? Why allow what appears to be needless suffering on the part of the incarnate One, if that suffering could be avoided? In Boso's words:

> If God were unwilling to save the human race
> except in the way which you have described,
> when God could have done it by a simple act of will,

do you not see how, to say the very least, you disparage
   God's wisdom?
For if someone without any reason for doing so,
does with great labor something that could be done with
   ease,
such a person would not be judged to be wise.
Regarding your statement
that in this way God shows how much he loves you,
this doesn't make sense,
unless it can be demonstrated that humanity could not be
   saved
in any other way. (S. II, i, 54–55)

This question posed a serious problem for Anselm. Even
though he was presenting his position with Christ out of the
picture, so to speak, there was nonetheless the fact which he
knew and could not ignore, namely, that the Incarnation had
taken place. Since it is axiomatic for him that God always acts
in ways that are in keeping with divine wisdom and goodness, Anselm had to show that simple forgiveness on God's
part, which at first thought might seem appropriate to us, was
not in keeping with God's plan for human creatures. Anselm is
forced into this position precisely because he knows as a matter
of fact that that was not the way God had chosen. If God did
not choose this way, it is obvious that it is not fitting: it is not
the way most in keeping with God's wisdom and goodness.

Anselm offers two reasons why a simple act of merciful forgiveness would not be fitting to bring about human salvation.
The first is that "if sin went unpunished, there would be no difference between the sinner and the nonsinner. This would be
unbecoming to God" (S. II, i, 69). Furthermore if disobedience
were simply forgiven, this would mean that the disobedient are
in effect not subject to any law. This Anselm explains would
make them like God, as the Devil had suggested to Adam and
Eve in the garden.

His second reason has to do with the honor of God and the
order of the universe which God created. The creatures God
made give honor to God when they maintain, either in a natural
way or (for humans) by reason, the order according to which the

universe was created. Sin dishonors God, because it strikes at and disrupts that order. This is fundamental to Anselm's thinking. I need to point out, however, that we must be careful not to interpret dishonor done to God in an overly anthropomorphic way, as if to think that because of sin God experiences outrage or insult or hurt feelings. In no sense can sin dishonor God in God's very being. What it does dishonor is the order and harmony of God's creation. It mars the beauty of the universe. A most significant part of that beauty is the beauty as God's human creatures in their state of original blessing.

This vision that the beauty of the universe is defaced and disfigured by sin is of great importance to Anselm. As Southern points out, "beauty" is a new word in Anselm's vocabulary. It does not, however, refer "to poetic or pictorial beauty, but to the beauty of a perfectly ordered universe."[6] Simple forgiveness on God's part would not repair the harm done to the order of the universe. In fact, simple forgiveness would leave that disorder uncorrected and the beauty of the universe unrestored.

Perhaps a simple example may help to clarify what Anselm had in mind. Several years ago I gave a valuable icon to the Abbey of Gethsemani. It was an icon of Mary seated on a throne with Christ sitting on her lap and looking out from the icon. I had been able to obtain this strikingly beautiful icon while in Greece. At the abbey it was placed on the wall of the entrance to the abbey church from the retreat house. It was wired to the wall so that no one could make off with it. One night a woman from the area, who was known to be somewhat deranged, came into the retreat house, and for some reason decided to take down all the paintings in the retreat house and place them on the floor. When she came to the icon I had donated, she found herself frustrated because it was wired and she was unable to take it from the wall. Finally, she pulled on it, broke it in two and then carefully laid it on the floor. A work of beauty had been defaced. In Christian compassion, one could forgive her for her misdemeanor. But forgiveness would not restore the beauty of the icon.

I am sure you see the point I am trying to make. I realize of course that, like all comparison, this one limps rather badly.

---

6. *St. Anselm: A Portrait in a Landscape*, 212.

Thus, the woman is in no way involved in the beauty of the icon, whereas humans are a very significant part of the beauty of the universe — that beauty which human sin defaces. The link with Anselm's argument is the fact that, while she can be forgiven, forgiving her would in no way restore the beauty of the icon. I want to say, for those who might be distressed by this story, that a well-known artist actually did restore the icon.

The point of the comparison is that, like the woman who defaced the icon by her intemperate action, humans have by sin disfigured the universe of which they are a part. As in the case of the woman, human persons can be forgiven their sin; but forgiveness alone leaves the order of the universe still in disarray and its beauty seriously marred. Even freely given divine forgiveness, therefore, does not remove the dishonor that sin brought to God's good creation and, therefore, to God.

Anselm offers a similar comparison.

> Think of a rich man who has in his hand a precious pearl
> which is in no way defiled
> and which cannot be taken away from him unless he
>   permits it.
> He decides to place it in his treasure chest
> which contains things that are very dear and most precious
>   to him. . . .
> Suppose he allows some envious person
> to strike it from his hand and cast it into the mud,
> though he could have prevented this;
> and then afterward he puts it, soiled and unwashed, into his
>   treasure chest.
> Would you consider him a wise man? (S. II, i, 85)

> [Anselm addresses this question to Boso, who dutifully
>   replies:
> How can I?
> For it would make much more sense
> to keep and preserve his pearl clean than to have it polluted.]

At this point you, the reader, may be exasperated with Anselm (or with me or with both of us). You might feel inclined to say: "Come now, Archbishop, you are making matters so complicated. Why can't God just forgive and as part of that forgiveness restore the universe to its original beauty? After all, if God was able to create an orderly and beautiful universe by a word, why can't God just as easily restore it? You seem bent on making up unnecessary problems for God."

Such a reaction is surely understandable. What it does not take into account is Anselm's unrelenting commitment to the simplicity of God and to the unity in that simplicity of divine justice and mercy. Justice demands that humans must make reparation for the dishonor done to God. Mercy calls for compassion and forgiveness for one who is frail and weak. Does this create an impasse? For mercy cannot set aside justice, nor can justice override mercy. This problem is one that Anselm had struggled with before: how to put mercy and justice together without sacrificing one or the other. Years before in the *Proslogion* he had wrestled with this problem. There he says:

> Although it is difficult to understand
> how your mercy is not lacking in your justice,
> still I must believe that it is in no way opposed to justice,
> since it flows from your goodness,
> which is not goodness without justice.
> This means that mercy and justice are in harmony with one
>   another.
> For, if you are merciful because you are supremely good
> and cannot be supremely good unless you are supremely
>   just,
> it must follow then that you are merciful
> precisely because you are supremely just. (S. I, 108)

It may be that you have trouble with these words whereby Anselm makes the goodness of God the "common denominator" of his mercy and justice. It is perhaps heartening to realize that Anselm himself had difficulty with his own words! In fact he continues the prayer (and I am quoting from the *Proslogion*, which, you will remember, is one long prayer for divine light) with an appeal to God for help.

Help me, O just and merciful God,
whose light I seek, help me,
so that I may understand what I have just said:
namely, that you are merciful precisely because you are just.
(Ibid.)

Thus, in the *Proslogion*, Anselm asserts the unity of justice and mercy in God, but in the process prays that he may have the light to understand what he has asserted. We may well decide to join him in praying that we too "may understand what [he has] just said," namely, that justice and mercy are one in God. The CDH is an attempt to illustrate this assertion. Southern in his careful analysis of Anselm's "predicament" stresses the importance of rectitude. Rectitude is simply the right order of things. Rectitude is present when things are what they ought to be. The right order of things demands that human beings, having placed themselves in a state of sinfulness, should be forever deprived of eternal blessedness. This is the demand of justice. Yet the right order of things equally requires that human beings, created by God for everlasting happiness, should achieve the end that God intended when God created them. Anselm puts it this way: "It is necessary for God, on account of his unchangeable goodness, to bring to completion what God has begun in his human creatures" (S. II, ii, 5). This would be to go the way of mercy.

There are, therefore, two ways of dealing with humans, both of which flow from the right order of things. It should be noted, though, that God's intention, destining humans for eternal blessedness, is antecedent to human sinfulness. Therefore, paradoxically, God's justice has to say "no" to eternal happiness for humans, but it also has to say "yes." This is to say that divine justice somehow enfolds divine mercy. Thomas Merton put it this way: "[God's justice] is God's fidelity to the reality which is His creation and which reflects His hidden Being."[7] Or as Anselm says in his prayer to God in the *Proslogion*: "You are merciful precisely because you are just."

---

7. Thomas Merton, *Dancing in the Water of Life: The Journals of Thomas Merton*, vol. 5, 1963–1965 (New York: HarperCollins, 1997), 19.

Try to see it this way: *justice* demands that humans — because of their state of sinfulness — be forever deprived of the happiness of eternal life. But *justice* equally demands that God's original plan — that humans enjoy everlasting blessedness — not be thwarted. That is why it must be said that *God's justice demands mercy*. This insight flows from what Thomas Merton calls "a profoundly contemplative view of God's plan for man and for the cosmos." Merton continues:

> [Anselm] takes with the greatest seriousness the evil of sin as an injury and dishonor to God's love for us, as our Creator and Father: but we must ascertain precisely what Anselm means by God's honor. The traditionally accepted language of sin as "outrage" and "insult" to God must not be interpreted too exclusively in an anthropomorphic sense.... He does not make any undue use of images that suggest wounded or outraged "feelings" on God's part, as if God were an extremely sensitive and vulnerable human. The injury done to God strikes at God, not in His being, but in the order and harmony of His creation, and the reparation of this injury must consist first of all in a restoration of the violated order willed by God in His wisdom and love.[8]

R. W. Southern has pointed out how Anselm's conviction that justice demands that God's original plan for humanity cannot be vitiated by human sin seems to place him in an awkward position. "From being impossible that sin should be forgiven, it now appears impossible that it should *not* be forgiven."[9] For if sin is not forgiven, humans will be deprived of the blessedness that God originally intended for them. But this cannot be, for God's designs cannot be frustrated even by human sin. Why then should not the forgiveness that Christ gained be extended to all humankind? To quote R. W. Southern:

> Anselm was here in a considerable difficulty. God's plan required that Man should be saved. This may mean either

---

8. "Reflections on Some Recent Studies of St. Anselm."
9. *St. Anselm: A Portrait in a Landscape*, 214.

"the species Man" or "all men." According to the first meaning, God's plan would be fulfilled by the salvation of a single representative of the race. According to the second, the damnation of a single individual would frustrate the intention of the Creator. Of these two possible meanings Anselm seems logically to be committed only to the first, and this would agree with his general tendency to think of the species as more real than its individual components. But though the salvation of one man may conceivably satisfy the logical requirements of his system, this could scarcely satisfy the requirements of God's mercy, since there is no logical objection to the benefit of the Savior's offering being extended to all whom he chooses.[10]

In the last chapter but one of the CDH Anselm speaks of the "value of Christ's death which far exceeds the magnitude of all the sins of men and angels." Again we may ask: does this not suggest universal salvation? Already in chapter 19 of book 2 of the CDH, an interesting exchange between Anselm and Boso had highlighted this very issue. Anselm quotes the Nicene Creed: God became flesh for us and for our salvation. The "us" in "for us" and "for our salvation," Anselm says "are those whom he calls his brother and sisters."

How very appropriate, then, that,
when he beholds so many of them weighed down by so
    heavy a debt,
and wasting through poverty, in the depths of their miseries,
he should remit the debt incurred by their sins.
And give them what their transgressions had forfeited?
                                          (S. II, ii, 130)

Boso expresses his wholehearted agreement: "The world can hear of nothing more reasonable, sweeter, more desirable. And I experience such confidence from [what you say] that I cannot

---

10. Southern, *St. Anselm: A Portrait in a Landscape*, 214.

describe the joy with which my heart exults." Boso then proceeds to pose the issue for which Anselm had no immediate answer: "It seems to me that God can reject none who come to him in his name." Anselm's response is weak: "It is so, if the person comes aright." And the Scriptures tell us how to come aright, he suggests. He realizes, however, that more needs to be said, but he is not the one to say it. He confesses: "There are doubtless many reasons which are beyond me and which human understanding cannot grasp" (ibid.).

"Which human understanding cannot grasp" — yes, at least not yet. But after all, the discipline of theology ("faith seeking understanding") is an ever-growing way of understanding. Each age of thinkers opens doors to rooms which they themselves cannot enter, but which they leave open for another age to explore. Anselm was a person of his age: he believed, as did many of his contemporaries, that those who are saved are the few. Yet his refusal to give a definitive answer to Boso's question about the possibility of universal salvation opened a door, impossible for him to pass through, that made it easier for future believers to reflect about, and perhaps move in other directions on, this important issue about salvation. As Southern says of the conclusion of the CDH: Anselm "allowed the dialogue to end on a note which he himself could not echo."

> It is a very striking fact that, just as he had allowed Boso to lay the foundation for his main argument at the start, so he allowed him the last note at its end. He did not endorse Boso's hope, but in leaving it he allowed it to stand as the sign of the approach of a new and more hopeful age.[11]

The CDH ends with words of confidence and a sense of achievement. Boso's final words are:

> All the things which you have said seem to me to be reasonable and incontrovertible. Through your solution of the one question which I proposed I have come to understand

---

11. *St. Anselm: A Portrait in a Landscape*, 216.

the truth of all that is contained in the New and Old Testaments. For you have proved that it was necessary for God to become human [and have done so in such a way] that, setting aside the few things you have introduced from the Bible (namely, your remarks about the three persons of the Trinity and about Adam), you have satisfied not only Jews but also pagans [and have done so] by reason alone. This same God who became human in Jesus constituted the New Testament and confirmed the Old. Thus, just as it is necessary to affirm (*confiteri*) that he is true, so no one can deny (*diffiteri*) as true what is contained in these books.

Anselm speaks the final word and it seems to be a confident word:

If what we have said needs to be corrected, I will not refuse to do so, if the correction is a reasonable one. But if that which we think we have discovered by reason is confirmed by the testimony of the truth, we must attribute this not to ourselves, but to God who is blessed forever. Amen.

(S. II, ii, 133)

Meditation on Human Redemption

In 1099, the year after he completed the CDH, Anselm wrote a meditation on human redemption. It is surely the greatest of his meditations and is usually published with the earlier prayers and meditations he wrote. It is a wonderful complement to the CDH and for this reason may fittingly be discussed at this point.

In the course of a conversation with himself, with God, and with Christ the mediator, he sets forth in a tone that is highly personal the teaching which he had developed in a more speculative way in CDH. He begins the meditation by calling himself or any Christian to joyful meditation on wonders of the redemption wrought by Christ.

> O Christian soul, reborn from a death so grim,
> redeemed and freed from wretched slavery
> by the blood of God,
> arouse your mind,
> remember your rebirth,
> realize that you are redeemed and made free.
> Call to mind the power that wrought your salvation
> and whence it comes.
> Turn toward it in your meditation,
> discover its delight in your contemplation.
> Throw off your lethargy,
> strengthen your heart,
> direct your mind.
> Taste the goodness of your Redeemer,
> be on fire with love for your Savior.
> Chew the honeycomb of his words,
> suck their flavor which is sweeter than sap,
> swallow their wholesome sweetness.
> Chew by thinking,
> suck by understanding,
> swallow by love and rejoicing.
> Be glad to chew, thankful to suck, joyful to swallow.
>
> (S. III, 84)

Following this call to prayer, he invites the Christian to re-flection on the strength of Christ, the good Samaritan, who brought about our redemption. That strength that sets us free is found in the nail-pierced hands of Jesus. A mysterious strength, surely, that comes in the guise of weakness. A hidden strength, whereby one man's death on a cross takes away the burden of eternal death that lay upon the human race. Reflection moves him to prayer:

> Why, O good Lord, holy Redeemer, powerful Savior,
> why did you conceal such power in such humility?
> Was it to deceive the Devil,
> who by deceiving Adam and Eve
> had driven them out of paradise?
> But surely truth deceives no one.

A person who ignores the truth or does not believe it
deceives himself.
One who sees the truth and hates or despises it
deceives himself.
Truth deceives no one....
You assumed human nature
not to hide what was known of you,
but to reveal what was not known.
True God and true man you declared yourself to be
and manifested [that you were what you declared] by what
  you did.
This is indeed mysterious in itself, but not made so by
  intent....

What a wonderful statement of the meaning of the Incarnation: Jesus is the revelation of the ineffable God. He assumed human nature, not to conceal who he was but to reveal who God is. He reveals God by what he does. In his actions we can see God who in Jesus became human that humans might become divine.

Continuing his meditation, Anselm turns briefly to the atonement theory that had come down from the tradition. He asks whether or not the Incarnation was kept secret by God so as to deceive the Devil and trick him into acting in such a way that he lost all rights over humankind. Anselm's answer is clearly: No! God owes nothing to the Devil. Humans owe nothing to the Devil either, except to reverse the defeat that sin had brought about. For Anselm the ultimate reason for the Incarnation was that God willed it. And we can see the fitness of God's willing it this way:

God had no need to save humankind in this way,
but this was the way humans needed to make atonement to
  God.
God had no need to suffer so arduously,
but this is the way in which humans needed to be reconciled
  to God.
The divine nature was not obliged, indeed not able,
to suffer humiliation and to labor.

All these things needed to be done for human nature
that it might be restored to what it was meant to be.
But neither human nature nor anything that was not God
could bring about such restoration.... (Ibid.)

Anselm stresses the heinousness of sin. It dishonors God, not in God's essential divine nature, but in the disorder it produces in God's good creation. Satisfaction must be made, but it can be made only by one who is without sin and who can give to God (1) what that person does not owe and (2) what is more valuable than all that is not God. Clearly there was no way that humanity in its fallen state could meet these requirements.

God's goodness intervened:
The Son of God assumed human nature
so that in his person divinity and humanity would be united.
This person had what was greater than all things other than
   God.
He assumed the debt that humans ought to pay.
This he did, though himself owing nothing,
so that he could pay for others
the debt they owed but could not pay....
He who was not obliged to suffer death
and who could in all justice have avoided it
freely underwent it for the sake of justice....
He did not succumb to violence
but freely accepted it for the honor of God
and the good of humans.
He was not forced to do so out of obedience,
but in a manner altogether praiseworthy and merciful,
he willed it so in the power of his wisdom. (Ibid.)

Anselm proceeds to undercut the misunderstanding of his theory of atonement as it is so often presented, namely, that an angry God required blood to placate the demands of divine justice. Thomas Merton writes: "The *Meditatio* is perfectly clear that the death of Christ on the Cross was not intended to assuage a supposed divine thirst for vengeance.... The mystery of the Cross is something far deeper than this: it is a mystery

of love in which justice and love are seen to be not opposed
but one in the infinite holiness of God. And this, indeed, is the
divine honor in its highest sense: for an honor that would be
fully restored by a mere exercise of force would not be worthy
of an infinitely wise and loving God. His transcendent honor is
satisfied not by punishment alone but by reconciliation."[12]

> For the Father did not order him to die,
> much less compel him to do so.
> But understanding what was pleasing to the Father
> and good for humans,
> he acted of his own free will.
> Thus did the Son freely obey the Father,
> when he chose to do freely
> what he knew would please the Father.
> But, since it was the Father who gave him this good will
> (which yet was free), it makes sense to say
> that he accepted it as a command from the Father. (Ibid.)

In this way Anselm explains how the Scriptures can say that
"Christ became obedient unto death," but this obedience was
his own free choice. There was no compulsion. What was pleasing to God in Christ's death on the cross was not so much
the shedding of blood, but the supreme generosity of the love
which his free obedience manifested. A modern Welsh poet,
R. S. Thomas, has put this understanding into striking verse in
a poem called "The Coming":

> And God held in his hand
> A small globe. Look, he said.
> The Son looked. Far off,
> As through water, he saw
> A scorched land of fierce
> Colour. The light burned
> There; crusted buildings
> Cast their shadows: a bright
> Serpent, a river,

---

12. "Reflections on Some Recent Studies of St. Anselm," 228.

      Uncoiled itself, radiant
      With slime.

      On a bare
      Hill a bare tree saddened
      The sky. Many people
      Held out their thin arms
      To it, as though waiting
      For a vanished April
      To return to its crossed
      Boughs. The Son watched
      Them. Let me go there, he said.[13]

Anselm tells us that "because of that which was done on the cross, by the cross our Christ has redeemed us. Whoever wills to come to this grace with the love it deserves will be saved." At this point Anselm calls upon the Christian to rejoice in the salvation that had been gained for him or her by the death of Christ.

    So, Christian soul, here is the power of your salvation,
    the cause of your freedom,
    the price of your redemption.
    You were in bondage;
    but you have been bought back.
    You were a slave;
    now you are free;
    an exile, you have been brought back,
    lost, you have been found,
    dead, you have been restored to life.
    Chew this, bite into it, suck it,
    let your heart swallow it.
    And when you receive the body and blood of your Savior,
    make it in this life your daily bread.
    For it is through this and only through this
    that you will remain in Christ and Christ in you,
    and in the life to come your joy will be full.

---

13. R. S. Thomas, *H'M* (London: Macmillan, 1972), 35.

At this moment in the meditation Anselm asks himself how he can really rejoice when he reflects on the terrible cruelty that Christ underwent to save us from our fallenness. He is clearly writing in an age that had begun to reflect on and grieve for the sufferings that the Lord Jesus endured in his passion. The joyful recipient of redemption must look on the bleeding body of the Man of sorrows.

This long meditation on redemption moves toward its conclusion with an expression of gratitude to the Lord:

> You have set me upright
> and raised me to the knowledge and love of yourself.
> You have given me the confidence that my soul will be saved,
> for you have given your life for [my salvation]
> and have promised me your glory if I follow you.
> And when I was not following you,
> But was still committing many sins which you had forbidden,
> You waited for me to follow you
> Till you could give me what you promised.

Anselm reflects on how much he owes to God. It is a debt he can never pay, for he owes more than his very self.

> Lord, because you have made me,
> I owe you all of my love;
> because you have redeemed me,
> I owe you all of myself;
> because you have promised so much,
> I owe you all that I am.
> Moreover, I owe to your love so much more than myself
> just as you are so much greater than I,
> for whom you gave yourself,
> and to whom you have promised yourself.

The meditation, though deeply emotional, has been an exercise in reason coming to understand what faith believes about Jesus: his Incarnation, his suffering and death on the cross. This movement from faith to understanding is a basic principle of Anselm's theological method. But understanding is never the final goal. Love is. Therefore, moving from faith to deeper understanding, Anselm begs that that understanding may, in turn, be transformed into love. "I pray you, Lord, make me taste by love what I taste by knowledge; let me know by love what I know by understanding." The meditation soars to a bursting crescendo:

> I owe you more than my whole self, but I have no more,
> and by myself I cannot even return the whole of it to you.
> Draw me, Lord, into the fullness of love.
> I am wholly yours by creation;
> make me all yours, too, in love.
> Behold, Lord, my heart is before you.
> Admit me into the inner room of your love....
> Good Lord, do not reject me.
> I faint with hunger for your love; revive me with it.
> May your gracious care embrace me,
> your affection enthrall me,
> your love overwhelm me!
> Take me and possess all that I am.
> For with the Father and the Holy Spirit,
> you alone are God, blessed to ages of ages. Amen.
>
> (S. III, 84–91)

Thus the "Meditation on Human Redemption" ends on a profoundly contemplative note. It draws us into an intuition that threads its way through the teaching of Christian mystics from the beginning to the present — from the Gospel of John to Gregory of Nyssa to John of the Cross to Thomas Merton — the realization that understanding must finally yield place to love. It is only when understanding is coupled with love that we catch glimpses of God. As Thomas Merton put it: "When the mind admits that God is too great for our knowledge, love replies: 'I know Him.' "[14]

---

14. Thomas Merton, *The Ascent to Truth* (New York: Harcourt, Brace, 1951), 296.

A Brief Note on the Sacraments

Anselm wrote no *Summa Theologica.* The scope of his writing was confined pretty much to the truths expressed in the creeds of the church, and even for the creeds he did not feel the need to discuss all that they contained. Thus, he says practically nothing about the church or about eschatology and little about the sacraments. There are a few letters that refer to the sacraments. I discuss them here as a kind of appendix to the study of Anselm's understanding of why Christ became one of us.

As archbishop of Canterbury, Anselm set about enforcing the decrees of Pope Gregory VII concerning the celibacy of the clergy. In the year 1102 or 1103 he received a letter from Bishop Herbert Losinga seeking advice on what he should do about priests who refused to give up the women they were living with. Anselm makes clear to him that under no circumstances should such priests be allowed to continue to exercise their ministry. If other priests can be found, then let them act in the place of the recalcitrant ones. If other priests cannot be found, then

> monks are to say Mass for the people and consecrate the Body of the Lord, which should be carried to the sick by clerics. By your command and as your representatives, these clerics should hear confessions, give absolution and bury the dead. You may give all these faculties to monks of an advanced age, until the stubbornness of these priests is softened by the grace of God. (*Letters,* 2:242)

It will not be till the century after Anselm that Peter Lombard (1100–1160) will fix the number of sacraments as seven. Clearly in Anselm's time there was still something of a fluidity about the sacraments and also about ministry. It is undoubtedly true when he refers to monks being called to "say Mass" for the people, he is talking about monks who are ordained priests. But when he speaks of monks of an advanced age being granted these faculties he seems to be referring to both the saying of Mass and the giving of absolution. Are these "monks of advanced age" also ordained? It is not clear from

174 ♦ *Part Two: The Spirituality of St. Anselm*

the text. It is also of interest in today's world, where there is a shortage of ordained priests, to read that clerics (who certainly were not ordained) are empowered to hear confessions and give absolution.

Among Anselm's prayers, there is one to be said by the priest before receiving Holy Communion. The custom of inserting private devotional prayers of the priest within the liturgy became a common practice in the Gallican liturgy. Anselm's prayer may have been used for this purpose, or perhaps it was a prayer said by the priest before celebrating the Mass. It is worth noting that it is much more restrained in emotion than most of his other prayers. It draws heavily on the Scriptures, especially passages from St. Paul (Romans and Ephesians). Noteworthy is his linking of the eucharistic Body of Christ with the Body of Christ which is the church. Equally noteworthy is his clear understanding of an aspect of the Eucharist that is often forgotten, namely, that it is a sacrament of reconciliation: it brings about forgiveness of sin and offers protection against sinning again. The existence of a sacrament of reconciliation should not obscure the fact that the Eucharist is and always has been the primary sacrament of reconciliation. And even more: the Eucharist is a foretaste of the life of blessedness that will come with the final resurrection.

Lord Jesus Christ,
at the will of the Father and with the cooperation of the Holy
     Spirit,
you have, by your death and of your own free will,
redeemed the world from sin and eternal death.
I adore you, I venerate you,
as much as I can,
though my affection is halfhearted
and my devotion so feeble.
I thank you for so great a gift:
your holy Body and Blood,
which I desire to receive
for my own repentance
and as a safeguard against sin.
I confess that I am so unworthy

even to approach [this sacrament]
and touch [your Body and Blood].
But with confidence in the mercy by which you gave your
    life
to justify sinners,
and because of your goodness in offering yourself
as a sacrifice to the Father,
I presume, sinner though I am,
to receive this [sacrament]
that through it I may be justified.
As a suppliant, I beg you, source of mercy for us humans,
that what you have done to destroy sin
may not be for me an increasing of sin,
but rather forgiveness and protection.
Make me so to perceive with my lips and in my heart
and so to feel with faith and love
that, by the power of this [sacrament],
I may be deemed worthy to be planted
in the likeness of your death and resurrection,
through the death of the "old humanity"
and the renewal of the life of righteousness.
Thus may I be worthy to be incorporated
into your body which is the church,
so that I may be your member and you my head,
so that I may remain in you and you in me.
Finally at the resurrection
you will refashion the body of my mortality
according to the body of your glory,
as you promised through your apostle [Paul]
and I shall rejoice in you forever
to your glory,
who with the Father and the Holy Spirit
lives and reigns forever and ever. Amen. (S. III, 10)

Besides this prayer, one letter has been preserved which is entitled *Epistola de Sacramentis Ecclesiae (Letter Concerning the Sacraments of the Church)*. But, while the title is in the plural, it is only the sacrament of the Eucharist that is discussed; and then the discussion is largely about rubrics. The letter is a response to a letter from Walram, bishop of Naumburg (Germany).

Bishop Walram was bothered by the diversity he saw in the way in which the Eucharist was being celebrated. Celebrations differed from one place to another. What, he wanted to know, did Anselm think about such diversity? Anselm replies first by offering a general principle and then discussing the particular issues which Bishop Walram had raised. The general principle he enunciates is a fair one. He sees unity of practice desirable; but where differences do not compromise the fundamental realities of the sacraments, he would allow room for diversity.

> Certainly if [Eucharist] were celebrated in one way and with one mind throughout the church, this would be good and praiseworthy. There are, however, many differences which do not conflict with the fundamental importance of the sacrament or with its efficacy or with faith in it; and these cannot be brought together in one practice. I think, therefore, that these differences ought to be harmoniously and peacefully tolerated rather than be disharmoniously and scandalously condemned.

Anselm makes clear that in enunciating this principle he is simply citing an approach to diversity that has long won acceptance in the church. Thus he continues:

> We have it on the authority of the fathers that, provided the unity of charity is preserved in the Catholic faith, diversities of administration are not harmful. If you ask where these diversities of customs come from, I can only say that they arise from the diversity of human opinions, by which it happens that what one judges more suitable, another sees as less so.

He offers as his conclusion: "I do not believe that to disagree concerning such differences is to wander from the truth of the matter."[15]

---

15. Hopkins and Richardson, *Anselm of Canterbury*, 3:246–47.

I hasten to say that the differences Bishop Walram raised could hardly be thought to prejudice the importance or the efficacy of the sacrament. One of the differences he speaks of concerns the number of signs of the cross that presiders make over the elements of bread and wine: some make one sign of the cross over each element, some make several. Now at the Last Supper Jesus blessed first the bread, then the wine: thus only two blessings, would this not indicate what should be done? Anselm's reaction is that it doesn't really matter, one way or another. This problem posed by the bishop of Naumburg has to do with relating the Eucharist to the Last Supper. Anselm tells Bishop Walram that in the Eucharist it is not necessary to follow exactly what Jesus did at the supper. Indeed, if he did so, then to be logical, he would have to consecrate the chalice only after a supper meal. For the Gospel says that "after the meal" Jesus took a cup of wine in his hands.

The other problem the bishop brings up is concerned with relating the Eucharist to the sacrifice of Calvary. Some put a covering over the chalice from the beginning of the Mass, but others left it uncovered. The reason Bishop Walram advances for keeping the chalice uncovered is that Christ was crucified naked. Anselm, perhaps decrying an understanding of the Mass (which actually developed fully in a later age) — an understanding that would find parallels between the ritual of the Mass and the events of the passion — finds either practice regarding the covering of the chalice acceptable. For, he tells this rather scrupulous bishop, if you try to image in the liturgy the events of Jesus' passion, then you would have to celebrate outside of any building and outside the boundaries of a city, because Christ was crucified under the open sky and outside the city walls.

Finally, Anselm's pastoral advice is that the best place to look for parallels to Jesus' sufferings and passion is in the way we live our lives. A most important insight, surely, for liturgy has little meaning if we fail to bring to its celebration the imitation of Christ that goes on in our daily lives. Liturgy is an expression of who we are and what we hope to become. It's about life, not just about correct ritual.

The fundamental issue of diversity and unity in worship

much occupies the Roman Catholic Church in this period of the church's life at the end of the century and the beginning of a new millennium. The issues under discussion are far more important than the number of signs of the cross or the covered or uncovered chalice. They are issues that relate deeply to the meaning of the Eucharist and the meaning of a eucharistic community.

As the number of priests available to preside at Eucharist continues in rapid decline (through retirements, deaths, the drying up of vocations to the priesthood), there exists in the church a diversity of opinion about what ought to be done. What is the proper procedure if a priest is unable to be present for a Sunday Eucharist? Should parishioners be advised to go off to a neighboring parish? Or should they preserve the unity of their parish community and celebrate a liturgy of the Word, with someone, properly deputed, leading the celebration? Or have we reached the time where more radical solutions need to be examined, such as widening the possible pool of candidates for the priesthood?

As Anselm says: some judge one way more suitable; others, another. But he also says that no judgment is acceptable if it compromises the importance or the efficacy of the sacrament. It may well be that we are in the uncomfortable ecclesial situation in which we have opened doors, but are not yet comfortable about which door we need to enter. Only time and listening to the Word of God as it speaks to us in myriad ways will bring us the light to know.

Conclusion

The Joy of Faith

Anselm's dialogue is actually for Boso and himself. . . . His purpose is to increase, by reason, their Christian joy in revealed truth. Intelligible joy is regarded by Anselm as one of the characteristic fruits of monastic study and prayer. The understanding which faith attains by meditation, study, prayer and intuition stands half-way between the obscure assent of faith and the pure light of the beatific vision. — THOMAS MERTON

This book, as I stated in the introduction, had its beginnings with a visit to a bookstore in Canterbury, when I first laid eyes on R. W. Southern's *Anselm and His Biographer*. It traces my own journey through the wonderful world of Anselm's thought and prayer: a journey that I have invited the reader to take with me. For me it has been a fascinating, even exciting journey, if not always an easy one. I hope that you, the reader, have shared that fascination and excitement, even as you also may have found that the path through his writings was not always easy. But we can agree, I hope, that it was always a path worth traveling.

Making a new friend is always a joyous experience, even if you get to know him or her only through writings. The experience is especially remarkable when one has to span centuries to meet this friend. The Anselm I have come to know is a gracious and gentle person whom his friends loved and loved to listen to, a bold and innovative writer who challenges his readers with new ideas, a holy man with undaunted faith and a courageous willingness to submit that faith to reason's scrutiny. He had his priorities straight and never swerved from the course on which he set his life when he became a Benedictine monk. There is a prayer in the Roman missal which asks: "may we use well the things of earth and love the things of heaven." This prayer embodies a Benedictine understanding of spirituality. It sums up Anselm's. Life is a journey. He was a pilgrim with eyes ever trained on that journey's goal: the heavenly homeland. What he prized most of earthly existence was friendship. For in his eyes friends were fellow pilgrims on that heavenward journey, and friendship was the one reality of time that survived in eternity.

Last year at the beginning of Lent, I suggested to the congregation with whom I celebrate liturgy that some enterprising person might design a Lenten vest. One side of the vest might be purple, the other side gold. Each side of the vest would have a pocket in it. In the purple pocket, there should appear a card with the message: "I am dust and ashes." In the gold pocket the message on the card should read: "I was created for glory." This, I believe, is what the Lenten liturgy is about: on the one hand, I am a creature totally dependent on God, full of mortality, and a sinner to boot; on the other hand, I was made for God and for eternal happiness in God. The paradox of living the liturgical season of Lent, and indeed of living the Christian life as a whole, is to deal in creative tension with the paradox of the two poles of the human reality: our deep-down nothingness and our glorious destiny.

I doubt if Anselm would have known very much about vests, but I do believe he would have identified with the understanding of the human condition which the "vest project" implies, namely, the striking contrast between human littleness and human greatness. These two ways of looking at the human person run through the *Prayers and Meditations*. Anselm may begin a prayer with a deep consciousness of his abject sinfulness, but invariably his prayer ends on a note of optimism: based not on his merits, but on the goodness of God.

These two approaches to the human reality are deeply enshrined in the text of the CDH. God in divine love has destined God's human creatures for beatitude, for sharing the divine life. But a wayward streak in humans defaults on God's plan: human persons become sinful, fallen creatures who have, seemingly irretrievably, forfeited the wondrous destiny God had planned. But God's plan cannot be ultimately thwarted. God's love must prevail. The fabric of the divine plan, unraveled by sin, is beautifully mended and restored by Jesus Christ, who is God become one of us. Divine love, which destined us for eternal happiness, wins out by restoring to us what sin had lost.

These two truths — human fallenness (caused by human infidelity) and human greatness (willed by God, lost by sin, restored by the Incarnation) are rock-bed realities of Christian faith. For Anselm they were also truths that can be supported by human reason.

Since Christianity's beginning, Christian thinkers have reflected on the relationship of faith and reason. Tertullian, the brilliant Carthaginian lawyer of the second century, was wary of such a relationship. His dictum: "what does Jerusalem have to do with Athens?" translates into: what does revelation have to do with human wisdom, what does theology have to do with philosophy, what does faith have to do with reason? Tertullian's response was unequivocal. His *credo quia impossibile* (I believe because it is impossible) makes clear that for him faith has nothing to do with human wisdom. The many times in which fundamentalism in diverse forms has made its appearance in the ongoing narrative of the Christian story testify to the fact that Tertullian's rejection of any bridge between "Jerusalem" and "Athens" has scarcely ever been without a following. More than that, there have been those who joined him in denying the link between "Jerusalem" and "Athens," but who parted company with him in the choice he made. Where he chose "Jerusalem," they chose "Athens." Religious stances that grew out of the Enlightenment opted for a religion of reasonable ethics that left no room for revelation. For the leaders of the Enlightenment "Athens" had nothing to do with "Jerusalem."

While Tertullian does indeed stand at the head of a tradition that has persisted through the centuries, it would be a mistake to see it as the major tradition in the continuing Christian story. His extreme *credo quia impossibile* was, ultimately, no match for Anselm's more moderate and more reasonable *credo ut intelligam*. Most Christian thinkers have attempted to establish a link between revelation and human wisdom, between faith and reason. At times the attempts have been clumsy and the marriage of "Jerusalem" and "Athens" a precarious or unhappy bond. At other times the marriage has been a congenial one and has produced healthy offspring.

Early Christian writers, like Origen, Clement of Alexandria, Augustine, and so many others, did not hesitate to use Plato and Plotinus, even when their theologizing was largely commentary on the Sacred Scripture. But, as we have seen throughout this book, Anselm went beyond them, using logic and dialectics to talk about the truths of revelation, and therefore employing reason to articulate those truths more explicitly. He was convinced that he could "prove" the truths of faith by necessary arguments drawn from reason. As I have pointed out, "necessary reasons" for Anselm often meant reasons of fitness. It was his firm conviction that God would never do anything that was not befitting to the divine being. On the other hand, if it was befitting that God do something, then that is what God would do.

Reason and faith, he stoutly maintained, had to be compatible, since both came from God. Use reason rightly and understand faith correctly and there is bound to be accord between them. Still it must never be forgotten that faith is able to stand securely on its own. As M. J. Charlesworth has written:

> If Anselm wishes to reserve a place for reason, he is at the same time equally concerned to emphasize the autonomy of faith. In other words he wishes to say that faith is possible without any kind of prior rational preparation or justification. The Christian believer, as he constantly says, can (indeed must) believe before he understands.... As Boso says [at the beginning of the CDH]: "I have come not so that you should remove doubts from my faith, but that you should show me the reasons for my certainty (of faith)."[1]

Thus, while Anselm uses reason to prove faith, he is quick to assert that reason does not give a greater certitude to faith. The greatest theologian and the simplest person of faith have the same certitude. For such certitude comes from God who

---

1. Charlesworth, *St. Anselm's Proslogion*, 33–34.

gives the gift of faith. What, then, does that deeper understanding that comes with reason add to faith? One of the consistent themes of this book has been simply this: that understanding enhances the inner, radiant beauty of faith and heightens the joy that one already experiences in believing.

Perhaps the two important truths our age can learn from Anselm are his absolute confidence in the faith he professed and the joy he took in that faith as he reflected on it, wrote about it, and meditated on it. An age of seekers and doubters, like our own, may well be ready to listen to Anselm. He is a wise, warm-hearted, and personable icon of the Joy of Faith.

A Tribute

Lanfranc, with all his great qualities, lived and died among us as a stranger. His worthier successor, from the moment when he first set foot on our land, won the rank of an adopted Englishman by standing forth as the champion of the saints of England. Stranger as he was, he has won his place among the noblest worthies of our island. It was something to be the model of all ecclesiastical perfection; it was something to be the creator of the theology of Christendom; but it was something higher still to be the very embodiment of righteousness and mercy, to be handed down in the annals of humanity as the man who saved the hunted hare and stood up for the holiness of Alphege.*

---

*Edward A. Freeman, *The History of the Norman Conquest of England,* vol. 4 (Oxford: Clarendon Press, 1876).

Bibliography

The Latin Texts

Schmitt, F. S. *Sancti Anselmi Opera Omnia.* 6 vols. Edinburgh: Nelson, 1939–61; reprint: 2 vols. Stuttgart: Friedrich Frommann Verlag, 1968.

Schmitt, F. S., and R. W. Southern. *Memorials of St. Anselm.* London: Oxford, 1969.

Translations

Charlesworth, M. J. *St. Anselm's Proslogion.* Notre Dame, Ind.: University of Notre Dame Press, 1979.

Deane, S. N. *St. Anselm: Proslogion, Monologion, Cur Deus Homo.* La Salle, Ill.: Open Court, 1903; reprint 1954.

Eadmer. *Vita Anselmi (The Life of St. Anselm).* Latin text with English trans. R. W. Southern. London: Oxford, 1972.

———. *History of Recent Events in England (Historia Novorum in Anglia).* English translation only, by Geoffrey Bosanquet. London: Cresset Press, 1964.

Fröhlich, Walter. *The Letters of St. Anselm of Canterbury.* Kalamazoo, Mich.: Cistercian Publications, vol. 1, 1990, vol. 2, 1993, vol. 3, 1994.

Hopkins, Jaspers, and Herbert Richardson. *Anselm of Canterbury.* 3 vols. Lewiston, N.Y.: Edwin Mellen Press, 1974–76.

Ward, Benedicta. *The Prayers and Meditations of St. Anselm with the Proslogion.* London: Penguin, 1973.

Secondary Sources: Books

Anselm Studies, An Occasional Journal. White Plains, N.Y.: Kraus International Publications, vol. 1, 1983; vol. 2, 1988.

Barth, Karl. *Anselm: Fides Quaerens Intellectum*. Trans. I. W. Robertson. Richmond, Va.: John Knox Press, 1960.

Chittister, Joan. *The Rule of St. Benedict for the Ages*. New York: Crossroad, 1995.

Evans, Gillian R. *Anselm and Talking about God*. London: Oxford, 1978.

———. *Anselm and a New Generation*. London: Oxford, 1980.

———. *Anselm*. Wilton, Conn.: Morehouse-Barlow, 1989.

Hopkins, Jasper. *A Companion to the Study of St. Anselm*. Minneapolis: University of Minnesota Press, 1972.

Knowles, David. *The Monastic Order in England*. Cambridge: Cambridge University Press, 1949.

———. *The Evolution of Medieval Thought*. New York: Vintage, 1962.

Leclercq, Jean. *The Love of Learning and the Desire for God*. New York: Fordham University Press, 1961.

Leff, Gordon A. *Medieval Thought from St. Augustine to Ockham*. Chicago: Quadrangle, 1959.

Loughlin, Sr. John David. *St. Anselm as Letter Writer* (Catholic University of America dissertation). Ann Arbor: University of Michigan Press, 1968.

Luscombe, D. E., and G. R. Evans. *Anselm: Aosta, Bec, and Canterbury*. Sheffield, Eng.: Sheffield Academic Press, 1996.

McIntyre, John. *St. Anselm and His Critics*. London: Oliver and Boyd, 1954.

———. *Rule of St. Benedict*. Collegeville, Minn.: Liturgical Press, 1981.

Schufreider, Gregory. *Confessions of a Rational Mystic: Anselm's Early Writings*. West Lafayette, Ind.: Purdue University Press, 1994.

Southern, R. W. *The Making of the Middle Ages*. New Haven, Conn.: Yale University Press, 1953.

———. *St. Anselm and His Biographer*. Cambridge: Cambridge University Press, 1963.

———. *St. Anselm: A Portrait in a Landscape*. Cambridge: Cambridge University Press, 1990.

Secondary Sources: Articles

Feiss, Hugh. "The God of St. Anselm's Prayers," *American Benedictine Review* 36 (March 1985): 1–22.

Fiske, A. "St. Anselm and Friendship," *Studia Monastica* 3 (1961): 259–90.

Merton, Thomas. "Reflections on Some Recent Studies of St. Anselm," *Monastic Studies* 3 (1965): 221–36.

————. "St. Anselm and His Argument," *American Benedictine Review* 17 (June 1966): 238–62.

Pacht, Otto. "The Illustrations of St. Anselm's Prayers and Meditations," *Journal of the Warburg and Courtauld Institutes* 19 (1956): 68–83.

Schufreider, Gregory. "A Classical Misunderstanding of Anselm's Argument," *American Catholic Philosophical Quarterly* 66 (1992): 489–505.

Southern, R. W. "Anselm and His English Pupils," *Medieval and Renaissance Studies* (Warburg Institute of the University of London) 1 (1941): 3–34.

Vaugh, Sally N. *Anselm of Bec and Robert of Meulan: The Innocence of the Dove and the Wisdom of the Serpent.* Berkeley: University of California Press, 1987.

crossroad

Benedict J. Groeschel
AUGUSTINE
Major Writings
0-8245-2505-1; $13.95

Renate Craine
HILDEGARD
Prophet of the Cosmic Christ
0-8245-2510-8; $14.95

Harvey Egan
KARL RAHNER
Mystic of Everyday Life
0-8245-2511-6; $16.95

Robert Barron
THOMAS AQUINAS
Spiritual Master
0-8245-2507-8; $14.95

William Griffin
C. S. LEWIS
Spirituality for Mere Christians
0-8245-2506-X; $14.95

Please support your local bookstore, or call 1-800-395-0690.
For a free catalog, please write us at
THE CROSSROAD PUBLISHING COMPANY
370 LEXINGTON AVENUE, NEW YORK, NY 10017

We hope you enjoyed Anselm: The Joy of Faith. *Thank you for reading it.*

crossroad